ACCIDENTAL HEROD

BECOMING A LEADER YOU CAN LIVE WITH

By David McNitzky

A Quarry Press Publication

QUARRY
PRESS

AUTHOR: David McNitzky
EDITOR & DESIGNER: Kathrin DePue
LOGO DESIGN: Ben Toalson
COVER PHOTO: Jason Train,
https://www.flickr.com/photos/98004108@N03/9195944224

CONTENTS

ACKNOWLEDGEMENTS

~

The important activities of the Christian life, like mission and discipleship, require community. Though not as significant as those activities, this book required community as well.

I want to acknowledge and thank the communities whose contributions have been invaluable in communicating this story. I must start with my favorite community: my wife and three sons. Pam, Mark, Ryan, and Reed have lived through both the orphan and heir days of my life. They always provided a safe home and acceptance from which I can work, though I did not always realize it.

The pastors at the Alamo Heights UMC staff were also crucial in this story. Their wisdom, giftedness, and sense of humor help keep me going. It is a constant privilege to work with Burky, Donna, Dinah, Scott, Michael, Linda, Robert, Mark, and Matt. These pastors are joined by other pastor-types every Tuesday to discuss the text for the upcoming week. These Tuesdays are soul stretching and energizing for me.

I'm also blessed to have taught an outstanding group of lay ministers at the Quarry on Thursday nights. That is my favorite night of the week. Darrell and Stacy Smith, Quarry alumni, played large roles in this book's development. Darrell wrote most of chapter eight, and Stacy helped me find my editor and publish this book. One of the things we like to say about our Alamo Heights family is this: "When you get one of us, you get all of us." I am grateful to have all of the pastors, Quarry, and AHUMC staff, as well as all the others in my life and ministry.

I'm grateful to the congregations of Los Fresnos UMC, Helotes Hills UMC, and FUMC Boerne for loving me through my orphan days. I cannot imagine doing the family business without my spiritual family at the Alamo Heights UMC. Their default position has always been to support their pastor. I hope I can match their level of grace, wisdom, and commitment to Christ.

Finally, I'm grateful to my editor, Kathrin DePue. It was her talent, creativity, and passion that made this book a reality. Any shortcomings in the book are my responsibility and not hers. She did the best that she could with what was given to her!

-David

INTRODUCTION

"Come to me all you who are weary and burdened and I will give you rest."

~

The people I hang out with are a tired, angry, and anxious lot that is often gripped with disappointment and guilt. You may be thinking, "He needs a new group of friends," but I hang out with some of the best people in the world. My friends are pastors and church leaders, just like me. *Tired* is the first word that comes to my mind when I think about our group. My friends are not afraid of hard work. Quite the contrary: they work extremely hard—probably too hard. Their tiredness may not stem from all the effort they exert; rather, this constant near-exhaustion likely stems from the reality that their tireless efforts seem to yield so few results. They work harder every day to keep from losing ground when not working at all would produce a result only vaguely worse.

It is easy enough to see, through statistics and anecdotes, the lessening influence of the Christian church in North America. We visit this topic often enough in our conversations; we tire ourselves further by assessing the success or failures of our efforts as leaders of the church; and we are pulled into a constant cycle of initiation, execution, and heart-crushing evaluation. Why do we continually choose to make our home there?

When tired people see little fruit from their hard work, anger, and frustration will follow as naturally as the Four Horsemen follow one behind the other. This reality is best illustrated in a discussion I heard about a pastor whose office overlooked a busy freeway: he positioned his office in this way because he wanted to see something move that he didn't first have to push. Too often, we, as leaders, have pushed with all our might only to find that our exertion failed to move the object forward and instead made it roll back and nearly crush us.

In my capacity as a head pastor, I have pushed my faith community to be seeker driven (sensitive and purpose driven) and missional. This effort has been met with resistance and confusion from many congregation members and general apathy from a world in chaos. I have tried hard...*really* hard...and I live with an underlying anger that is commensurate with the extent of my failed efforts. The more I try and the fewer positive responses I receive from others, the more my anger threatens to consume me.

This constant anger is passive in nature; it does not often unearth itself onto others. It is likely to result in a general sense of sadness and despair, or it will cause me to seek something to numb that pain (e.g., food, television, internet, or dreams of something different). For some of my colleagues, this anger pops up like the proverbial beach ball held too long beneath the surface of the water and causes regrettable damage to their reputation and their personal relationships. If I cannot take my anger out on the community I serve, I will take it out elsewhere—likely in a place where I least wish to cause pain.

We also tend to be very anxious. If our efforts continue to fail, what will become of the faith we love so much? What will happen to our place in the world—not just as an institution but also to those of us who are in leadership for the institution? Declining numbers, shrinking funds, and lessening influence: not exactly a recipe for job security. The church often mirrors its leaders' anxiety. We live in an extremely anxious world; fear about the economy, terrorism, the future for our children, and the direction our world is heading surrounds the average

American churchgoer. Add to that list the fear of the changes being made within the church, and the anxiety level rises even higher. If you cannot count on your faith and religious institution to remain stable, what can you count on?

All of our exhaustion, anger, and anxiety must come from a source. There is surely someone to blame for all of this. The leader too often concludes that she is the one to blame, and in rides the most devastating of the Four Horsemen: *guilt*—and not the kind of existential guilt that leads to repentance; it is a sense of shame and utter unworthiness in the face of so much seemingly fruitless effort. This guilt stems from *what we do*, but it produces a sense of shame in *who we are*. Guilt says, "I made a mistake," but shame says, "I am a mistake." For many leaders, anger is more self-directed than directed towards the unresponsive community.

Thankfully, we church leaders are a resilient bunch. Where many would run away or quit after just a taste of this shame, we often turn up the intensity of our efforts instead. We try even harder, we tire ourselves even more, we increase our anxiety, and we become even angrier at our situation and ourselves. In his book, *Ordering Your*

Private World, Gordon MacDonald urged leaders to consider whether they are called or driven to the efforts they undertake. Many of the well-meaning leaders with whom I serve in the kingdom seem *driven*. The madness is not only alive in the Don Drapers in the advertising world of the 1960's; madness is prevalent in church leadership circles as well.

This 'madness' bothers me for a number of reasons. First of all, I do not like to be in or see other leaders in so much pain. It is heartbreaking to watch people I deeply care about drive themselves into the ground, harm their families, and wound their communities...all "in the name of Jesus." Secondly, this madness in no way reflects the gracious invitation Jesus gave to his followers when he told them to find rest in him. *Rested* is not a word I often use to describe the modern church and her leaders. Thirdly, this kind of driven behavior is a lousy witness to our communities of faith and to the world. Who wants to join a group of tired, angry, anxious, and guilty Christians? People are interested in and attracted to Jesus, but, like Nietzsche, they may have issues when his bride looks "leprous." Lastly, this driven-ness bothers me greatly because it is unnecessary. It is not the life to which Jesus has called us; it does not bring rest to our souls, order to the world, or shalom to the chaos around us.

I write this book for those in church leadership who are 'driven'—not because I have all the answers but because I have had a number of wrong answers. One day when I looked introspectively at my leadership and at the congregation of the Alamo Heights United Methodist Church under my leadership, I realized I did not look like Jesus. I looked like King Herod the Great. Herod was more than a baby killer; he was successful, rich, culturally relevant, powerful, and pragmatic, and he built some awesome structures. We as a church were chasing these seemingly "good and faithful" things (the pragmatism, the cultural relevance, the wide-reaching influence, etc.). But we were driven, and I could not find rest for my soul.

Around the time I started my journey at AHUMC, theologian Marcus Borg published a challenging book called *Meeting Jesus Again for the First Time*. Here, I ask pastors and Christian leaders to meet Herod "again for the first time." I want to share Herod's journey and my journey with you. I want to examine how we both went off track and offer you the hope he never found—a hope that I found. In telling my story, I see God's role in it anew. I hope my story will illuminate God's role in yours as well, and I pray that you too may find rest for your soul.

CHAPTER ONE

Meeting Herod Again for the First Time

~

One of the wonderful, half-a-century-old traditions at our church is the annual Live Nativity. The church used real animals until the year a donkey broke loose and cruised down one of the main thoroughfares of our city. By the time I came to Alamo Heights United Methodist Church in 1995, we were using live people and stuffed/cardboard-cutout animals. The first few years I took part in the event, I intentionally played the part of the wicked King Herod. It seemed a fine irony: the new, kindhearted pastor playing a baby-killer Herod. The real irony would only become apparent several years later when I began to play Herod in real life. Don't fear: I did not order the massacre of any babies. To the contrary, I supported the expansion of our nursery and the hiring of more staff to help supervise small children. But there was far more to Herod the Great than his decision to kill babies in order to protect his crown. Herod turned out to be much more relevant to my world than I wanted to admit.

For reasons perhaps known only to God, Herod is a major part of the Jesus story even though Herod dies when Jesus is young. Herod's sons (also named Herod—an ancient George Foreman-type family legacy) ruled during Jesus' adult ministry. Nevertheless, Herod's legacy was so profound that he continued to be an undeniable force and a recognizable influence long after his death. Herod was named "King of the Jews" by the Roman Senate at age thirty-three. A Roman official independently bestowed the same title on Jesus, when Jesus was also thirty-three, before he went to Calvary. Further, Jesus and Herod's son Antipas are in both direct and indirect contact throughout their adult lives. Some scholars even postulate that Jesus moved his base of ministry from Nazareth to the Sea of Galilee shortly after Herod Antipas moved his headquarters from Sepphoris, a few miles from Nazareth, to Tiberius on the Sea of Galilee. Herod, and his legacy, was a part of Jesus' story, and he is also a part of my story and our story as church leaders.

I met Herod "again for the first time" in January 1999. I had the opportunity to travel to Israel under the tutelage of Ray VanderLaan. By that time, Ray had been leading groups to Israel for more than two decades. His research and experience led him to organize the trip around one major theme: the massive contrast between Jesus and Herod the Great. Our fifteen days in Israel that year introduced us to many of Herod's remarkable building projects. Near the end of our trip, Ray stood at the top of the Herodium, Herod's manmade mountain on which Herod built a large palace. Ray traced the roots of Herod and Jesus back to the Genesis struggle between Jacob and Esau; Herod was a distant descendent of Esau. Jesus, of course, fulfills the promise made to the tribe of Jacob, also known as Israel. This trip and Ray's presentation sparked my interest in this important figure who dominated his world and opposed the one God chose to rule the world. Like a child with a brand new Tonka truck, I enthusiastically used my new theological toy to give devotionals and talks on Herod and on Herod and Jesus. I looked through stacks of material written by Ehud Netzer, the primary authority on Herod in Israel. But I quickly forgot about my new toy and moved on to my next area of interest. I no longer played Herod at the live nativity; I began playing a shepherd (talk about a whole different kind of irony!).

Then, in 2007, I got a second opportunity to travel to Israel with Ray. The main theme of the trip was now, appropriately, the kingdom of God (that was Jesus' favorite subject, after all). Herod was still a prominent feature of the trip: we visited his famous mountain fortress, Masada, and we went to the Herodium. However, this time our activities on the Herodium revolved around those palace ruins. Rumor had it that Herod's long-lost tomb had been discovered by archaeologists working alongside Ehud Netzer. Though security was tight and we were not able to get close to it, the archaeological team allowed us a glimpse of Herod's supposed tomb. I remember Ray's excitement; he more fully appreciated it than any of the rest of us—including me.

Sure enough, in December of the next year, King Herod the Great gained minor celebrity status in the modern world. National Geographic magazine devoted its cover story to Herod and his tomb. Cable television aired a special on Herod, perfectly coinciding with the release of information about the tomb's discovery and with the annual rehearsal of "Herod and the wise men" scene in the Live Nativity. I remember thinking Herod would be pleased with all of this worldwide media attention. But then again, maybe not. Herod probably would've preferred to be named Time magazine's "Man of the Year," and he surely would have rather been on one of the major networks instead of the lowly cable TV channels! Most scholars agree that Herod set out to be the greatest builder who ever lived. He set out to be the greatest man in human history, and he almost did it.

Herod had it all. Herod had wealth, and lots of it. Scholars agree that Herod was the richest man in the world in his time. Ray VanderLaan guesses that Herod was richer in his day than Bill Gates is in our day. Where did all that wealth come from? Herod controlled the route tradesmen had to take in order to move spices and other goods from Arabia to the rest of the economic centers of the world. Herod was an Idumean from the desert area south of Israel; his family dealt in spices and could tax the spices that came through the areas that were under his family's rule. We can see a glimmer of the wealth of spice traders at the magnificent ruins of Petra in Jordan. These famous ruins were used as the setting for the final resting place of the Holy Grail in the movie *Indiana Jones and The Last Crusade*. To go from Arabia to Egypt, Asia Minor, or even Rome, spices and other goods had to pass through Herod-controlled lands on Herod-controlled routes. You want to trade with an Eastern power like Assyria, Babylon, or Persia? Pay Herod.

Ray VanderLaan also credits Herod's wealth to his control of the manufacture and distribution of a substance known as balsam. It was made in a super-secret facility in the desert near Qumran (where the Dead Sea Scrolls were found). This product was said to make the wearer of this perfume irresistible up to fifty paces way from members of the opposite sex. An ounce of this product sold for more than an ounce of gold! There was no concrete evidence of its supposed success rate. Yet people, Romans especially, bought it by the boatload. Herod built a great harbor at Caesarea Maritima on the Mediterranean Sea where he imported Roman soldiers to keep peace in his kingdom and exported his balsam to Rome. A visit to the ruins of this balsam facility reveals three distinct compartments of production; they were set up in that way so that no worker (no person outside of Herod's family) could know the entire recipe or process of producing the product—not unlike the way the recipe for Coca-Cola is known to only a select few. Herod was, among other things, a shrewd businessman.

Herod was so wealthy that he became a one-man economic stimulus package for Israel. Scholars estimate that Herod, during any one time of his reign, had anywhere from ten to forty percent of Israel on his payroll. He even occasionally paid the entire country's taxes to Rome. Furthermore, some of the most direct connections between Herod and Jesus came in the area of economics.

Jesus and his father were "Tektons." This Greek word has been translated as “carpenter.” It could also be translated to “stonemasons.” Herod’s son Antipas used stone from a very large quarry outside of Nazareth to build the Greek-inspired capital, Sepphoris, a few miles from Nazareth. Many Nazarene stonemasons worked on this project. It is not unlikely that both Jesus and his father were at one point employed by Herod's family. We even find out in Luke that "Joanna, the wife of Chuza, the manager of Herod's household" helped fund Jesus' ministry (Luke 8:3).

Herod also had power. With the help of his father, Antipater, he was named governor of Galilee in his twenties. With the help of the Romans, he was named King of Israel at the ripe age of thirty-three, and he successfully ruled for thirty-four years. That area of the world was extremely volatile in Herod's time; many religious factions and political groups fought for power and control. The Jews themselves were split into religious and state affiliated factions. Still, Herod capably ruled the land and kept the turmoil to a minimum—save, of course, a major revolt in 6 BCE that resulted in the death of thousands of Galilean revolutionaries. Jesus lived in the shadow of this event.

Herod keep order so effectively that the Roman Senate officially proclaimed him "friend of Romans," and he even returned the borders of Israel to those that stood under the reign of King David almost one thousand years earlier. Tom Mueller, in the National Geographic article, “The Real Herod,” published in December 2008, described him as "an astute and generous ruler, a brilliant general, and one of the most imaginative and energetic builders of the ancient world." Peter Richardson, a Herod scholar, notes in his book, *Herod King of the Jews and Friend of the* Romans, that Herod "rebuilt roads, expanded trade routes, collected taxes, and steered a course between rival sectarian groups in Judea."

He also had prestige. He was indeed the greatest builder of his time. I’m reminded of the great American architect, Frank Lloyd Wright, who, when called to testify at a trial identified himself as the "greatest living architect." When he got home, his wife chastised him for that arrogant remark and asked why he said it. Wright said, "I had to. I was under oath." Herod would understand Wright's statement, though he needed no legal incentives to tout his own greatness. His works witnessed to his greatness. Herod built seven palaces, each one larger than Caesar's palace (the one in Rome, not Las Vegas!). Most of his projects defy the typical or natural in some amazing way: At Caesarea, he engineered a manmade harbor; Masada was a palace fortress built in the desert by the Dead Sea on top of a mountain; he built palaces in Jerusalem, Jordan, and Jericho (as many as twelve palaces in all); and the Herodium is a Herod-made mountain. The Herodium is visible from the Mount of Olives, and some scholars speculate that Jesus had this particular mountain in mind when he touted faith's ability to move mountains in Matthew 17:20. Jesus' followers had actually seen a mountain move!

With his gold medal at the Olympic Games in Athens, Herod also held prestige as a star athlete. He subsidized the Olympics and became a lifetime patron for the Olympics; he was not only was a member of one of the most prestigious "country clubs" in the world—he was the owner! On the famous Acropolis of Athens, a statue of Herod was erected in recognition of and gratitude for his efforts. A second

Herod statue was erected at the Forum in Athens. His star status was surely only enhanced by the beautiful, famous, and desperate Cleopatra's attempt to seduce him. Though her efforts failed, Herod went on to have ten wives; he may well have died from a sexually transmitted disease. Were Herod a player in our time, he would surely have icon status greater than that of any athlete, politician, or billionaire; he was all three! As the 2008 National Geographic article notes, Herod's contemporary, Octavian, also known as Caesar Augustus, said that Herod was "meglio-psychic"—great of spirit. Octavian said Herod was, "too large to fit a small kingdom like Judea."

Like many famous and wealthy people, Herod sought to use some of his money and power for good. He was a philanthropist. He claimed to be supporting the common good, though I cannot help but wonder if these donations were meant to spread further his name and reputation. Like John D Rockefeller and Andrew Carnegie, who competed for the title of America's leading philanthropist two millennia later, Herod may have been trying to incur favor and fix any negative image he had in the public. Through Herod's efforts, pcople were employed, religious sites (for pagans, Jews, and emperors) were built, and a stable peace was secured. He was Michael Jordan, the Great Gatsby, John Wayne, Douglas MacArthur, and Warren Buffett rolled into one "meglio-psychic" force.

I should note here how Herod arrived and remained at this level of prestige and power—it is as impressive as that power itself. Firstly, Herod did not get to that point without some inherent advantages. Herod was born into a wealthy ruling family. His father, Antipater, was both an Idumean nobleman and a ruler of Judea appointed by the Romans. Antipater's influence situated Herod in a seat of power that allowed him to become governor of Galilee at a young age. Herod married into the only thing that passed for a ruling family in Judea: the Hasmonean family. This family was instrumental in gaining Judean freedom from the Greek rulers a century before Herod came to power. Herod's marriage to Mariamme united the Judean kingdom with the desert Idumean kingdom—giving Herod control of a very strategic piece of the Ancient Near East.

Through his family connections, Herod also had power over a land with great strategic, economic, and military influence. He also had "friends in high places": He was closely aligned with Mark Antony, the

Roman general who had the greatest influence over Herod's region. This friendship, of course, brought Herod to Cleopatra's attention. Later, after Antony lost the struggle for Julius Caesar's empire to Caesar's nephew, Octavian, Herod formed a strategic friendship with Octavian. Herod reminded Octavian of the close relationship he had with Octavian's rival, Antony, and with both his life and rule at stake, Herod promised Octavian that he would be as loyal to him as he was to Antony. Octavian was impressed with Herod's pledge, and in one bold stroke, Herod went from backing a loser to celebrating at the very center of the winners circle. Herod's rule was secure, and Caesar was well served by Herod, who managed one of the most turbulent areas of Caesar's Empire.

Herod combined these familial and friendship connections with his many talents to gain power and notoriety. Herod was a very pragmatic ruler. He would act in accordance with certain principles and violate other principles depending on the situation. He did everything for the advancement of his cause. Herod was a third-generation Jew, but he offered sacrifices to the gods of Rome on Capitoline Hill when he was named "King of the Jews" by the Romans. He even built a temple to Caesar Augustus. As Richardson notes, Herod was "more accommodating to Caesar Augustus than...obedient to Torah."

He spent almost forty years of his reign and much of his wealth rebuilding the second temple for the Jews in Jerusalem, but this task was not only for the good of the people. Herod had great economic incentive for this project. More than 500,000 pilgrims (tourists) flooded Jerusalem for Passover, and by building the temple (a place for these 500,000 pilgrims to worship), Herod showed again that he was a one-man economic stimulus package.

I have no doubt that he also invested in the temple as a way of incurring favor with Jewish leaders and keeping an uneasy "peace." Many Jewish leaders saw through this ploy and noted that though Herod constructed pagan temples for Rome and Caesar, he did not contribute to the building of a single synagogue. Herod even allowed a Roman symbol, the Eagle, to be placed on the temple. It was also assumed that Herod participated in the execution of the "freedom fighters"—Jews who scaled the walls of the temple to tear the pagan symbol off of Jerusalem's holiest site. Herod's conferred designation as "friend of the Romans" demonstrated his ability to maneuver easily among the winds of political change. Richardson notes that in accommodating the Romans, who guaranteed the solidity of his rule, he became "more Roman than the Romans."

One of Herod's most obvious characteristics was his addiction to scale and size. Everything Herod accomplished was done to the epitome of impressiveness. His manmade harbor at Caesarea plunged almost one hundred feet deep and had concrete forms set at the bottom of the sea. All of this was done without scuba gear! Next to this impressive harbor, Herod built a theater, which is still in use today, a palace, and a large hippodrome—a large arena where spectators could watch chariot races or gladiator contests. When flooded with water, the arena could even host a sea battle between large ships. When I first visited Caesarea in 1999, archaeologists estimated that the arena would have been able to hold 185,000 spectators. By 2008, they had increased that estimate to almost 300,000. This arena, which Herod built in the first century B.C., was three times the size of the Rose Bowl, which was constructed 2,000 years later. I do not doubt that the stadium was more impressive in its day than the new AT&T Dallas Cowboys Stadium is to today's most emphatic football fan—but there is no need to tell Jerry Jones that.

I've already mentioned Herod's manmade mountain the Herodium, on top of which Herod built a seven-story condominium palace. This palace could be seen all the way in Jerusalem—several miles away. The palace also contained the largest swimming pool in the world; it was so large that Herod built a tiny island in the middle of it. He could go out to his island and hold private conferences; would-be intruders had to take a boat to reach him in the middle of the pool. Water wings and life vests were of little use in that situation! This massive pool and private island speaks to Herod's narcissism and neuroses.

Herod's sense of scale is clearly seen in his best-known palace, Masada. In the desert on the Dead Sea, Herod devised an amazing water capturing system that would fill large cisterns in the Masada fortress with enough water to supply 1,000 soldiers for ten years. Seventy years after Herod's death, Masada became the perfect hideout for the zealots in their revolution against Rome. Netzer discovered that the zealots used the Herodium as a base as well. Herod's rule resulted in massive and finely furnished buildings and yet also sowed the seeds for destruction that came to fruition seventy years later (more on that in chapter three).

Then there was the most obvious symbol of Herod's attention to size and scale: the rebuilding of the second temple. The temple mount was the largest temple in the world—and in a world known for gigantic temples to pagan gods like Athena and Apollo. But Herod gave the Jews the largest temple of all. The internal dimensions of the temple were prescribed precisely by God in Scripture, so Herod could not do anything to change that. However, Herod could make the temple as high, the walls as thick, and the courtyards as large as he desired. Stones weighing as much as 570 tons were brought to the area to build both the temple and the mount on which the temple stood. Engineers still marvel at how Herod could have moved such large stones without the mechanisms available today. Josephus notes that the temple courts were six times larger than that of the previous temple area—a feat Herod accomplished through the artificial increase of the size of the hill by moving the stone of the hill itself. Thus, Herod constructed another manmade mountain.

Since only priests could work as construction crews on the temple, Herod employed 1,000 priests in that work. John 2:20 says the work took 46 years, but certain aspects of the work likely continued on for a total of 80 years. Unfortunately, less than a decade after it was finally completed, the Romans destroyed the temple during Titus' siege in 70 CE. Need an idea of how truly massive the temple was? While working twenty-four hours per day and seven days a week, it took Titus's men eighteen months to tear down this massive stone fixture. The "Western Wall" is all that remains today of Herod's most prized architectural achievement.

Herod is perhaps most known as the baby killer and perpetrator of cold, calculated violence. National Geographic, in its 2008 article, casts doubt on the biblical account that Herod massacred the babies of Bethlehem. The article claimed there is no historical evidence of that event, but allow me to cite some. We know that Herod killed his favorite of his ten wives, Mariamme. He thought she had conspired against him with one of his own advisors. He killed her teenage brother, Aristobulus, whose talents and abilities threatened Herod. He killed three of his own sons whom he saw as potential threats to or rivals for his throne. Two of those murdered sons were of Mariamme, men who would have been the most qualified to inherit his kingdom and rule it long after his death. Herod's three sons who did inherit the kingdom, Herod Philip, Herod Archelaus, and Herod Antipas, would have been more able to carry on the legacy of Moe, Larry, and Curly than the legacy of their powerful father. Herod killed one of his sons by roasting him over a fire during a dinner banquet; he stopped to rotate the young man at the "appropriate" intervals. Here was a man who could kill a few children, whom he was directly related to, but who were perceived as a threat to his throne.

It is also known that in the little hamlet of Bethlehem there were so few babies born that the massacre of the few who were born would not register with census takers and historians in their day. The King James Version of the Bible describes Bethlehem in such a way that it seems to have been barely large enough to have an ancient version of the Holiday Inn, much less big enough to be an epicenter of procreating Jews.

Herod was an equal opportunity killer: he killed senior citizens and babies; he killed peasants and priests. We know that Herod was responsible for the deaths of thousands of Galileans in the village of

Magdala in the tax revolt of 6 BCE. Herod wiped the entire city off the map. Many of the revolutionaries were burned alive when Herod commanded his troops to set fire to the caves on Mount Arbel where rebels hid. Many of Jesus' contemporaries saw their parents or grandparents hung to death on the doorframes of their own homes in the aftermath of this revolt as a warning to future Galilean revolutionaries. Herod also hammered an earlier peasant revolt of a group he called "brigands" in Galilee years before this most noteworthy incident—an act that first brought Herod to the attention of Roman officials.

As Herod neared the time of his own death, he knew he was not well loved by the Jews, so he ordered the round up and imprisonment of thousands of Jewish sages and officials in Jericho where they would be executed when he took his own last breath. Herod wanted to guarantee that the entire area under his rule would mourn on the day of his death. Mariamme's refusal to round up and execute this group led to her own death because Herod viewed this refusal as treason and took revenge against her. Thankfully, Herod's officials also refused to carry out his death wish for these respected men of Judea when Herod died in 4 BCE.

That, in a nutshell, is "Herod the Great." As Eugene Peterson says in *The Jesus Way*: "Herod was impressive. Herod was effective. Herod was successful. But Herod was also secular and godless" (206). What a description! It is certainly not any way I would ever want to be spoken of. Unfortunately, I ended up living into a vision and role of church leadership that threatened to make me into Herod the Great for the modern age.

CHAPTER TWO

Accidental Herod

~

In March 1995, just four months before I became the new senior pastor, I walked into the beautiful, newly completed, 1,200-seat sanctuary of our Alamo Heights United Methodist Church. Members of the church's personnel committee and the head of the building committee showed me around. Requiring more than a decade of planning and construction, and a mile and a half move from its original location, this new sanctuary's journey was part of the church's complete campus relocation. The labor this project necessitated may not have been obvious upon completion, but the fruits of that labor were universally observed. One neighboring pastor noted that this massive, thirteen million dollar effort would change the church landscape of the city of San Antonio and put AHUMC in the center of it all.

All were in awe of this simultaneous campus relocation and construction, except one person: me. As we walked through this magnificent cathedral, which could hold twice as many worshippers as the old building, I said to the head of the building committee, "This isn't going to be big enough." That was not the most appropriate thing to say to a person who had poured a decade of his life's energy and discretionary time into this God-honoring effort (he still reminds me every once in a while that, thanks to my leadership, it is still large enough!). While I was not particularly tactful, I was ignorantly truthful. I came to that arrogant conclusion honestly.

I had discerned a call from God into ordained ministry almost twenty years prior to that first visit to AHUMC. In an undergraduate class on American church history, I studied Walter Rauschenbusch and the social gospel movement of the late nineteenth and early twentieth centuries. I read about the church's involvement among the poor in the Hell's Kitchen area of New York City. I decided at that moment exactly what my life would be about: I would share the good news in word and deed among the dispossessed. In seminary a few years later, I found myself ministering to the Durham, North Carolina middle class. There were dispossessed in Durham, but I was not involved with them. I was instead involved with wonderful, loving church members who had significant needs of their own. Under the leadership of my wonderfully bright and pastoral mentor, Willie Teague, I began to understand that God needed me among the middle class just as much as the poor urban area needed Rauschenbusch. Walking with people through birth, parenting, divorce, illness, and death would challenge me and provide opportunities for sharing the gospel. I remember waiting with parents for a rebellious teen to come home. I remember calling on family members who were new to the church and were eager to deepen their faith. Most of all, I remember listening to stories of a couple who had lived through the Nazi bombings of London in the summer of 1940. These people mattered. The work was interesting and was not very difficult. I was the "student associate pastor"; budgets, policies, programs, and organizational concerns in general were not on my radar.

But all good things must come to an end. After graduation, I found myself appointed as the "pastor in charge" of a small-town church. Suddenly, there were reports to fill out, committees to run, and an organization to manage. I threw myself headfirst into the effort of building the organization. I worked as if the survival of the Hell's Kitchen people depended upon the success of the organization. And why not? Our organization accomplished good things; we provided opportunities to worship and grow spiritually; we educated children and youth in the faith; we even sent money to help the poor. My goal, though I would not have articulated it in this way at that time, was to help the organization grow and keep the people in the organization satisfied. I made a subtle move from concern for people to concern for the organization. Before long, I was running a church.

And I was running it pretty well, actually—so well, in fact, that the Methodist hierarchy saw fit to "promote" me to leadership in larger organizations. I was willing to be promoted; I was willing to break ties and make new ones in order to advance in my career. I wasn't a heartless mercenary: *If am serving God,* I reasoned, *it is more God-honoring to serve larger congregations.* I had a wonderful five-year tenure in my second church, but I soon left for a larger church. For the first time in my career, I was a "senior pastor." I was thirty-two years old (one year ahead of Herod's timetable), and it seemed like a big deal. I was also moving to one of the fastest growing counties in the state of Texas. I would work hard and the organization would grow in the years ahead; I assumed there was a correlation between the two.

People kept coming to the church, and I kept working to keep up with them. It seemed like a win/win; I worked hard and people responded. We both felt rewarded. It was not unusual for me to be away from home five to six nights a week visiting new members or sitting in on meetings for planning our new sanctuary.

Unfortunately, it was not all win/win. Two issues came to the forefront: first, I was ignoring my family. I can't even count how many times my wife put the children to bed alone. As I look back on those self-important days of mine, I realize I found it easier to stay at the office and play God than to go home to a family with young children and play husband and father. Further complicating the problem was the fact that I felt as though the growth of the church was concrete evidence that God was pleased with my workaholic ways. My wife also felt that confronting me about my work habits would be tantamount to opposing God's will for the church. Thankfully, her theology was corrected long before mine. I was drying dishes one night after dinner when my five-year-old asked me, "Dad, don't you have a meeting tonight?" I glanced at my wife with a look that said, "What is that about?" She did not hesitate to let me know: "We have learned how to run this house without you." Reality set in. I was not Walter Rauschenbusch sacrificing my life for the dispossessed; I was David sacrificing my family for the growth of an organization. My habits began to change over time. My wife says the birth of our third child also made a difference; spending time at home was then a matter of survival. We were outnumbered! If I did not go home regularly, there may not have been a home to go to at all.

A second issue became apparent around the same time. I attended a leadership conference in South Barrington, Illinois. Bill Hybels and the Willow Creek Community Church were effective in sharing their principles, mistakes, and lessons with the conference. It was then that I first came to realize all my efforts were aimed at people *inside* the church. Hybels described it in this way: "Your ministry is to keep the sheep in the pen. If you do well, you move to a larger pen with more sheep. If you keep doing well with larger pens, they will make you a denominational executive, and you won't have to mess with the sheep at all!" He nailed it; that was the exact path I was taking. I realized that almost none of my time and energy was spent on a real concern for people who were called "the unchurched." Like thousands of other conference attendees, I found Willow Creek's passion, commitment, and focus intoxicating. I was almost as impressed by the fifteen thousand people who came to Willow's services every week. I was taken by a renewed passion to reach others for Christ—scores of others!

I began to re-examine my personal ministry and the ministry of our church. I developed a personal mission statement: "to use my spiritual gifts of teaching, leading, and preaching to affect the greatest number of people in the greatest way possible" (hmm, where have I seen that adjective, "great," used before?). I led the church to make changes towards becoming more aware of people outside the church and towards making us more relevant to those people. We started a new worship service at 9:45 a.m. that we thought was more relevant to the community outside our congregation. I even went home before the new service each week to change out of a suit and into khakis. When that service ended, I would go back home again, put my suit back on, and cover it with a robe! New people began to show up; they made their way in to that "relevant" service. It was working! It was a new win/win: new people came, and I felt important and successful.

At the crest of that wave, I rolled into the sanctuary of AHUMC. I had visions of thousands of previously unchurched people filling that sanctuary—for Jesus, of course. When I began my pastorate there that summer, I enlisted others in this vision of a church attracting new people by the hundreds and thousands. I recruited a group of leaders to attend another conference at Willow Creek with me. The next year, I took them to Saddleback Church in California to see Rick Warren's, "The Purpose Driven Church" in action. Willow provided the motive for our efforts: "People matter to God." Saddleback provided the method with its baseball diamond analogy: people were taken through the "bases" of membership, maturity, and ministry and touched home with mission. We began an informal, contemporary, midweek service, after the example of Willow, and began to offer 101 and 201 classes in membership and faith development, after the example of Saddleback. In my second year, we started a "seeker-sensitive" worship service on Sunday evenings at 7:07 p.m. The 707 service was exciting with its culturally "in-tune" music and technology. We even offered an interactive question and answer session following each sermon. We were late coming to contemporary but early to emergent with this service! It was fun to watch the chairs in the gym fill up on Sunday evenings. I felt like a Bill Hybels, Jr.—never mind the fact that we are close to the same age. More people came. It was all good.

Unfortunately, not everyone was as enthusiastic about these changes as I was. Longtime leaders, including people who had made great sacrifices to relocate this eighty-five-year-old congregation, worried that I was trying to turn them into Willow Creek South or Saddleback East. They need not have been troubled; I may have learned the methods of Hybels and Warren, but I did not have the gifts to pull off their level of success. We were still about fourteen thousand shy of having fifteen thousand people at our weekend services. Nevertheless, I felt it necessary to hold a special weekend workshop for almost one hundred of our leaders in order to explain what Willow and Saddleback were about and the difference between them and our own proud and successful congregation. I thought their concerns were either evidence of a misunderstanding of my motives or evidence of their own narrow-mindedness. It would not be the last time I thought I knew better than my people only to discover they had God-given insight of their own that was far superior to mine. Years later, Shane Claiborne of *The Irresistible Revolution* would correctly diagnose my error. He noted that the problem with churches adopting Willow Creek's methods was that they did not have Willow Creek's history; they did not take the same journey. My leaders somehow knew that I was not only unfamiliar with the journey they had taken to get to where they were, but I was also trying to take them on someone else's journey. I could not see things from their view. I could only "see" all the hundreds of people who would come to our church because of my proposed changes.

But what would happen if they did not come? After a few months, the buzz about 707 wore off. A number of our regular attendees and members who had switched from the morning services or came in addition to the morning services began to move away from 707. We were eventually left with only thirty or forty people at the 707 service. These thirty-forty people were mostly members who did not come to our morning services; some were medical personnel who worked on Sunday mornings. We had succeeded in bringing new people to church, but I could not see that. I only saw the people who were no longer coming to the service. Though we succeeded in achieving our stated goal, we eventually removed the 707 service because we had not met our real, unstated goal: acquiring *many* new attendees and a feeling of success among church leaders. My repentance years later for the lack of vision that led to removing that service would not bring back those thirty to forty folks, most of whom we would never see again. I argued that lost people matter to God. What I really meant was, "Lost people in *large numbers* matter to God."

Regrettably, I used the same formula with the "found" people. During my first year, I lead a Bible study using the United Methodist's Disciple Bible Study. The twelve of us met weekly for two and a half hours to share our lives with each other over the Bible. Twelve was a good number for Jesus, but it was not large enough for me. I thought if I was supposed to influence the greatest number of people possible, I could not afford to spend this kind of time and energy on only twelve people. I ended my leadership in that group and began teaching a less demanding "pastor's study," which conveniently lasted only an hour. My reasoning seemed to be correct; more than one hundred people showed up for the study. But my hunch was also wrong; you cannot facilitate your influence on one hundred people in one hour a week. Fortunately, the twelve from that first study stayed together without me; for sixteen years, they shared all the challenges and joys of life together.

Despite my errors, the church continued to grow. After a couple of years, the 707 service was reborn under the leadership of a gifted new pastor, Scott Heare. It was called New Heights. With two Sunday morning New Heights services in the gym and three services in the sanctuary, attendance continued to increase. By 2001, we were fifty percent larger than we were in 1995. It was more win/win: a variety of worship experiences for a greater variety of people. They were pleased; I was affirmed. It is all good...if you didn't look at the man behind the curtain pulling every lever he could possibly find.

On September 11, 2001, the biggest lever was pulled from outside the church. The terrorist attacks that day generated an unbelievable amount of interest in our growing congregation. The local radio news station asked to interview me about the event; they were looking for any "spiritual" take I could offer them. Scott remembers the host asking me if I was nervous about having to preach on that coming Sunday to an unusually large number of people who were in deep emotional and spiritual crisis. I responded that I wasn't really nervous because there are people in our pews every Sunday who are experiencing emotional and spiritual crises. Of course, I knew I felt differently deep down. I even went to my study place in the Trinity University library to consult old magazines, journals, and books for sermons given after the Pearl Harbor attack. We had a Friday noon prayer service after September 11. The prophecy I made in 1995 about the sanctuary not being large enough came true for one day. I will never forget the arresting sound of more than one thousand people kneeling on the fold-down rails in the pews when we called for prayer. It looked like Easter Sunday. Long lines of worshipers waited to enter the sanctuary before the service and long lines waited to exit. I did not think much about the crowds that day; I focused on how we might find and deliver a message from God in the midst this crisis. However, I quickly began to fantasize about the crowds returning the next Sunday and every Sunday that followed.

At our membership height in 2001, we had multiple worship services: three on Sunday in the sanctuary, two on Sunday in the gym, and one midweek service in the chapel. We were the church equivalent of the movie theater: three different features at six different times. What's not to like about that? Everyone could surely find one of the six worship opportunities convenient to their schedule. We even felt that we were culturally relevant: our New Heights service featured a worship band, videos, and drama productions. We had great facilities, which were only six years old and the envy of other local churches. We would serve as host for one or two major conferences each year for our denomination or for other Christian groups. We had become like Herod the Great, by accident, of course. We were a well-meaning Herod, but we were a Herod nevertheless. I did not realize it at the time. I thought everything was good. *Look at all the people, programs, and resources we have!* I thought. *If some is good, more must be better. God must certainly be pleased.* Maybe there was some good in our efforts, but God was not as pleased with us as we were with ourselves.

It would take me a while to figure that out—a long while. In 2009, our church helped sponsor a conference for Renovare: an outstanding organization working for spiritual formation and renewal. The theme of the conference was "The Jesus Way." The title and theme were taken from a book by Eugene Peterson. In *The Jesus Way*, Peterson looks at how the life of Jesus was prefigured in several characters from the Old Testament, such as Abraham, Moses, and David. However, Peterson also investigates some characters who illustrate ways of life that are not the way of Jesus. The first character Peterson presents as a member of the latter group is…wait for it…Herod the Great. Peterson makes this observation while reflecting upon experiences from his teenage life on page 198: "I felt large and important. My adolescent imagination was being trained by Herod. I was immersed in a Herodian worldview where size and wealth defined the human condition." A bit later in the chapter on Herod, Peterson comments on the Roman way: "Herod reproduced that world of power, conspicuous consumption, and display on a smaller scale in Palestine. In reproducing it he was in no way inferior to Rome; in some ways he outdid Rome" (201).

Peterson's main objection to Herod's way of life is that it is largely impersonal. Jesus way is intensely *personal.* That is a point well worth reflection, especially as it relates to spiritual formation and discipleship. We will look at that idea later, but the immediate impact of Peterson's chapter was this: it made me begin to examine the parallels between Herod's approach to life and our church's approach to ministry under my leadership. The more I reflected on it, the more I realized that my ways had more affinity with Herod's ways than with "the Jesus way." I came up with twelve parallels at the forefront. That is a nice biblical number; but so is seven...and seven is a lot easier to count to! Here are the seven that came to me:

1. Success as the goal: Herod set out to be great. While I would not say I set out with the intention of being great, I did want our church to be important and successful. I liked the idea that we might become the center of the city's church geography. The sad truth is that Herod was a more able manager than I was, or else I might have achieved Herod-sized success. The fact that our church was a very large church but not officially a mega church was not due to any lack of desire on my part. To be sure, there is nothing inherently wrong with a "successful church," but that, in my opinion, should be a byproduct of the achievements of a well-managed church and not the main goal of that church.

2. Focus on size: Everything Herod did, he did on a large scale. Peterson was right; he outdid Rome. He focused on size when it came to people and buildings. Period. Even his temple remodel was aimed at serving a larger number of pilgrims. His punishments also focused on killing more rebels and, in the case of the roundup of respected men at the time of his death, innocent people. Herod knew that more was…well…more. With my opening and closing of Bible studies and worship services, I applied "the more" principle as the chief metric of evaluation.

3. Cultural relevance: Herod wanted not only to keep up with the "fashions" of Rome in building and politics, but he would even go so far as to set the trends. To be sure, the approval and respect of the Roman power and cultural elite was central to his political survival, but one assumes that he probably would've sought it even if his survival had not depended on it. Our church also wanted to be seen as "relevant" to the culture. I designed worship not only with God in mind but with the culture in mind as well. I liked reading our name in the local paper. I was *pleased* to have a few local celebrities, politicians, athletes, and wealthy citizens attend our services; and I was envious of churches who had more of any of those groups. I often felt we were one celebrity short of being relevant and, therefore, popular.

4. A community player: Herod wanted to be a key player in his world. He cultivated friendships and alliances that enabled him to court and exercise influence on the regional stage and the world stage. In many ways, Herod was a force for the common good in Israel. As we have already seen, he was a one-man economic stimulus package and a tax relief program. His able administration kept the Romans from decimating the population in that contentious, unsettled region. The religious establishment also benefited from his work on the temple. We too fancied ourselves community players. Our facilities provided needed gathering places for community events and space for large groups attending Christian conferences. Our architecture and presence helped clear the way for the development of the immediate geography around our church. We liked being pacesetters in the local community and in the Christian community at large.

5. Calculating behavior/pragmatism: Herod was ruthless and shrewd. He engineered buildings and relationships alike. Even his contributions to the Jews had political and economic motives. His marriages were no less calculated, though he deeply loved his bride, Mariamme, whom he married with the main goal of solidifying his rule of Judea. Our church also produced programs and services to attract and retain large numbers of attendees. Even the early membership classes I taught focused primarily on indoctrination into the church programs and were far less about becoming personally connected with the new members. The metric of "how many, how often, how much" was certainly used to analyze our work in our ministry planning circles. One drawback of our culturally relevant New Heights service was that the offering plate was nonexistent there. The two values of relevancy and calculation, which are usually complementary, clashed in that area. My Herodian psyche was torn.

6. *Disregard of "family"*: While Herod was not inattentive to the needs of his sister, Salome, he murdered other relatives and in-laws in order to do what he perceived necessary to hold fast to his throne. Herod's victims included his beloved Mariamme. According to scholars, he redrew his final will at least six times, and his lack of attention to and ineffective training of his heirs left his kingdom in shambles upon his death. While this sort of pragmatism was not a stated policy that I, or the church leaders, followed, I nearly "killed" my family relationships in my pursuit of my Herodian dreams for the church. Like Herod, I feared younger subordinates instead of looking for ways to help them gain strength, wisdom, and power of their own.

7. *Building a kingdom*: Herod was concerned solely with building and securing his kingdom. He literally built it with his

magnificent nature, his defying fortresses, and his carefully calculated political maneuvers. My church was about kingdom building as well. We thought we were building, of course, for God. However, we were doing the building entirely on our own rather than letting God build with us. That was not simply a gross theological mistake; it had disastrous consequences to the health of my soul, as we shall explore in the chapters to come. Secondly, it was actually *our* kingdom; we were calling the shots, and we would receive the glory. While we might claim to have had different motives and methods than Herod in this area, we were too close to his likeness for me to have any comfort in retrospect.

I would like to tell you that these insights in 2009 changed my leadership style, but, unfortunately, I changed more from feeling the heat than from seeing the light, as the saying goes. Fortunately, I quickly began to feel the heat.

CHAPTER THREE

A Herod-the-Great-Sized Crash

~

On my first trip to Israel in 1999 with Ray VanderLaan, I filled a bottle with Jordan River water and brought it home. No surprise there. More significantly, I also brought home a piece of smooth white marble from Herod's palace at Caesarea Maritima. The marble made the palace gleam; ships several miles away on the Mediterranean Sea could see the shine of the marble. In chapter 1, we saw that Caesarea contained the largest manmade harbor in the world, a 300,000-seat hippodrome, and a theater that is still in use today. But the theater is the only part of this massive Herod-architectural area that is still in use. If you look up "Caesarea Maritima" on Wikipedia you will find "ruin" under condition and "Israel Nature and Parks Authority" under owner. The palace and arena are crumbling. Tourists can still find pieces of palace marble along the seashore. According to the earliest Muslim account, the city was "reduced" when it was conquered in 638 CE. Herod no longer controls this ancient marble; it only exists in fragments.

My fragment, which I keep in my office drawer, reminds me of an important reality. It reminds me that everything Herod built fell apart. Not long ago, I watched the History Channel television series "Lost Worlds," which featured Herod the Great and his amazing palaces. They were stunning feats of architectural imagination in Herod's day, but today they belong to a lost world. Archaeologists have to search fragments for clues as to how the buildings once looked. The opulence of Caesarea and the Herodium are only visible as technologically generated graphics on computer screens. The years of digging that finally revealed Herod's tomb led only to the discovery that it had been smashed to pieces.

Herod's kingdom did not fare even as well as his buildings when his mostly inept sons took over. The Roman's split the kingdom in three and named Philip, Archelaus, and Antipas tetrarchs in the three sections. Under the not-so-careful watch of Herod the Great's descendants, rebellion replaced the peace that was once enforced by Herod. The Romans destroyed Jerusalem in 70 CE to wipe out the revolt of Jewish zealots in 66 CE. Another revolt led by Simon bar Kochba took place in Israel, and in 132 CE, Jerusalem was destroyed again and the Jews were scattered across the lands. Nothing that truly shows Herod's significance is left standing in the region Herod so ably ruled until his death in 4 BCE.

Herod's personal life was also a disaster. He had eleven wives, and he murdered his favorite. What was Mariamme's real crime? One story claims she was killed for treason. Some blame Herod's sister, Salome, who was jealous of Mariamme, for leading Herod to believe that Mariamme was unfaithful. Others note that Mariamme's royal ancestry led her to think herself capable of ruling in Herod's place; some stories claim she tried to poison Herod in order to free his throne for her rule. After having her executed, Herod built the statue of Mariamme and mourned her the rest of his days; he would call her name out as if to summon her from the dead. She filled his dreams, or, rather, his nightmares.

Herod spent the final years of his rule in stunning madness. Josephus, as noted in the December 2008 National Geographic article, attributed Herod's death to syphilis and gleefully listed Herod's symptoms: "internal pains and burning sensations, swelling of the feet, convulsions, a ravenous appetite, an ulcerated colon, worm eaten genitals, and very, very bad breath." We should note here that historians and storytellers of Herod's day often claimed that in His wrath, God inflicted God's enemies with syphilis. At any rate, Herod suffered greatly and likely died a gruesome death.

Herod knew that his death would not likely spark an outpouring of grief. Though Josephus suggests there was a great amount of respect for Herod visible among participants in his funeral procession, there was likely rejoicing outside of that procession. Many Jewish leaders were antagonized by Herod's Hellenistic ways and his calculated support of other gods. Many of the poor watched as Herod supported a system that allowed the Romans to acquired family plots if families did not pay their taxes and turn them into large-scale farms for the maximization of farming profits. The people of Judah saw Herod put down the local brigands before he came to the throne and kill protesters shortly before his death; he had the reputation of a mass murderer. The memory of Herod was so bitter that seventy years after his death he could still inspire acts of hatred. It is not surprising that Netzer found Herod's tomb in 2007 with the sarcophagus smashed into pieces—likely by Zealots who occupied the Herodium in the revolt of 66 to 70 CE.

Herod's knowledge and fear of this hatred may have been what led him to build his palaces in the first place. A map of the configuration of his palaces shows that they formed an escape route. From Caesarea or Jerusalem, he could escape to the Herodium, cross the wilderness to Masada, and end up at Machareus in Jordan. Each place was stocked with enough provisions and water for himself and his troops. He had been forced to flee for his life from rebels in 42 BCE as a young governor; he went to the Romans for help. The Romans gave him assistance and eventually named him King of the Jews. As King, he was determined to provide his own means of security.

This was probably not the greatness Herod envisioned for himself. I doubt that he dreamt of living in constant fear and eventually dying slowly in loneliness and depression. I'm sure he didn't plan to die a gruesome from illness. I'm certain he did not wish for his legacy to be mostly lost or destroyed upon his demise. Like Humpty Dumpty, Herod the Great had a great fall; he suffered a Herodian-sized crash.

It is not surprising that when I followed Herod in so many ways in my church leadership, I headed straight for his crash as well. I was teetering on the edge of my own wall. I described my feelings to my wife in 2004, and she thought maybe I just needed a vacation; but I was already too far gone for the help of vacation. I heard a colleague describe recovering from a heart attack during which time his church greatly reduced his workload and restricted his time at the office; I remember thinking, "Damn, that sounds good...except for the heart attack part." On November 1, 2004, I woke up, but I didn't hop right out of bed; I could not find the motivation to get up. I thought, "I'd like to be in the hospital and have people come visit me for a change." I wanted to be sick enough to go the hospital but not so sick that I could die or acquire serious or life-altering physical injuries. My thinking was not healthy. A trusted colleague suggested, non-judgmentally, that I take an online depression-screening test. I was not clinically depressed, according to the test, but something was very *off*. I had no energy and no real passion for the work I had engaged in so fully for years. I always looked forward to my time at the office each day...but I didn't then. I had to drag myself to the office on that day, the next day, and for the next four months after. I went. I soldiered on. I got by.

To say the least, I was scared. I tried to understand it. I prayed, I journaled, and I vented. I am embarrassed to say, I once wrote in my journal that I felt like one of the body-blockers for Col. Joshua Lawrence Chamberlain—a theologian and a hero of the Battle of Gettysburg. Chamberlain survived by hiding behind the bodies of dead soldiers, which absorbed the bullets for him. I wrote in my journal that I felt like I had taken on too many bullets for too many other people. It was a bit overdramatic, I admit. It was also wrong.

I eventually discovered that the majority of my wounds were self-inflicted, but at that moment, I was busy looking outward to identify where the bullets were coming from. Several things came to mind: My middle son had to have a shoulder surgery his senior year that ended his athletic career, and my Herodian-sized dreams for his athletic success were shattered. While I am fairly certain that athletic success mattered to him to a certain extent, it was clearly far more important to me. Secondly, the church had recently made an effort to raise money for a second campus called Riverside. I was hoping to raise $500,000 for Riverside by the ten-year anniversary at our location. My vision was not shared by the whole congregation, and the effort raised only $225,000. Though we ended up actually giving over $500,000 to Riverside, I was convinced that since my fundraising effort failed to meet my goal, it was a failed venture and I had failed Riverside. I felt like my congregation had let me down. The results were "not big enough."

This Herodian approach to the evaluation of results showed up in other areas of my leadership. My chronic frustration over the leveling-out of worship attendance on our main campus plagued me. After the high mark of 2001, our attendance rate slowed and actually began to go in reverse. I had never seen such a phenomenon in my 23 years as a pastor. If more members was better, then less members had to be worse. When my kingdom was built on size and success, leveling out looked a great deal like destruction.

For four months, I endured what many thoughtful people of faith have called “a dark night of the soul,” but my dark night was not like that of St. John of the Cross and other great people of prayer. I began to discover that my dark night was likely a consequence of my own actions and decisions. The wounds I experienced were largely self-inflicted. I set out on a Herodian quest to build a successful kingdom. In doing so, I made a couple of near fatal mistakes: I treated people as a means to an end. Though I have heartily endorsed the motto "lost people matter to God," I only valued them when they showed up, participated, and funded the organization I was building. What I didn't show in my leadership practice was this: attendees who did not participate were just as valuable as those who do. Jesus did not see crowds; he saw individuals. I was looking for crowds, and I often looked right by the faces of individuals.

I also thought the way to measure my value and worth as a pastor was by how many members came to my services and listened to my sermons (and for a time I truly acted as though they were *mine* and not the Lord's). If people responded, returned, and gave heartily, that meant that I was doing a good job and was a person of worth. It was bad logic, and it sucked the life out of me. I placed my self-worth entirely into the hands of other people. They never even asked for that responsibility; they couldn't (and shouldn't) have been trusted with that responsibility. One of my favorite quotes by Duffy Daugherty, Michigan State football coach, was in response to a reporter's question about the hardest part of his job. He said, "I am responsible to irresponsible people." He meant he could not trust the administration, fans, or reporters to assess his performance accurately. I eventually learned that I could not trust the people in my congregation (or myself) for an accurate assessment of my work, but in 2004, I was learning that lesson the hard way.

On top of all of this, I had the haunting sense that the feeling of darkness would never go away. If I could not pinpoint its cause, how could I expect find the cure? I thought I would have to stop being a pastor, and that thought haunted me even more. I didn't have a job when I was first out of seminary; I quickly discovered that having a master's degree did not guarantee me a job. I applied for a management position at a laundromat in Nashville, and I was told I was over qualified. My wife told me I could probably get a job driving an ice cream truck, but I didn't apply; I was afraid I would actually get that job! I discovered that my biggest concern in the job hunt had nothing to do with my personal economic status but everything to do with my personal identity. In 2004, after almost twenty-five years of identifying myself by my profession, I was terrified at the idea of no longer being a pastor. Who would I be? I began to think I needed a more marketable skillset to look for a new job (a new identity), but I really needed to rediscover my identity instead.

God graciously sent help my way. In England in January 2005, my friend Dorothy Vickers was doing her ironing when God told her I would come out of this wilderness by the end of February. She didn't even know I was lost. She passed that word from God to me, and I was encouraged. God knew what I was going through. Even though my current situation was technically "my fault," I would be delivered from it! My spirit was lifted in knowing God cared about me even though the kingdom I was trying to build "for him" was collapsing like a straw house in the breeze. Looking back on it now, I can't help but wonder if God was in favor of that collapse.

God was not finished. I began to receive some insight into what had happened in the church and what was happening now. I was led to the late Henri Nouwen, whose work I had read many times in the past, but this time his writing struck with new clarity. I began to realize that my identity was in my relationship to God as "the beloved," but I had been too busy listening hard for the voices of others to tell me who I was. Nouwen wrote, in *Home Tonight*, that we were created by God to be loved by God, our loving father—what Nouwen called "first love" (35). When we did not live in that love, says Nouwen, we look for "first love" from "second love" sources. I could almost hear the classic country tune, "Looking for love in all the wrong places," as I read. Since I live more from thought than from feelings, Nouwen's theological explanation for my wilderness experience helped me comprehend it more thoroughly. I expected from the congregation the love and acceptance that can only come from God. In my head, I understood where I went wrong that day; that understanding eventually made its way into my heart, but it took time to do so. It had not made it there by 2005, so I tried out a number of other "solutions" with the loving support of colleagues, friends, and congregants.

My first solution was geographic in nature. I took time away from work. I took a week of vacation in December 2004 and took a longer break in June 2005. This short sabbatical is called "renewal leave"—a four-week leave that a Methodist pastor is allowed every four years. After years of not using my renewal leave fully, I arranged to take this four-week break in addition to two weeks of my four-week yearly vacation time. I avoided doing anything that looked like work for six weeks. I still prayed and read the Scripture, but I did not go near our church. I took a graduation trip with my two older sons, who were soon to graduate college and high school, and my wife. I didn't do much besides that. I had two fears in taking this renewal leave: First, I was worried I would not want to go back to work. Second, I was terrified that the darkness would return and remain forever. While my fears were not unfounded, they were also not realized. I returned with renewed energy and a new perspective.

Another solution we devised to help renew my spirits was to make a change to my responsibilities. We decided that someone else would step up and take some of the bullets that would normally go straight into my chest. David Reed became Chief of Staff and took many of the front-line responsibilities off my shoulders. Slowly, I began to look less like a human Humpty Dumpty post-fall; I was being put back together. My pieces began to come back together, but some of the pieces that made up my being before my crash did not fit quite right. I was moving away from Herod-style leadership, which was characterized by my longing for extravagance and driven by the need to prove myself, but I was doing so almost unwittingly.

There is a story about a Cathedral in England that the congregation decided to dismantle in the onset of World War II in order to preserve the impeccable stained glass. Each family took a piece of glass home to hide and protect. When the war was over, each family uncovered its precious piece and put the church back together. Though the pieces did not fit together in quite the same way they did before the war, all agreed that the restructured cathedral was even more beautiful. The same thing happened to me.

As I continued to heal, I knew that one day I would be put back together and be better than I was when I crashed. One day I would see the key reason for my crash. One day I would understand Herod's faults, and I would understand myself better as well. One day I would experience the one thing Herod wanted most but never received.

CHAPTER FOUR

Homelessness: Haunting Herod and Driving David

~

One day in December 2012, I was in the Trinity University Library researching my new favorite topic, Herod the Great, and I caught a glimpse of a book on the table next to me. It was called *From Jesus to Christianity*. I realized the author, L. Michael White, was my son's professor at the University of Texas, and this book was one of the texts used for his class. I took a picture of the book and texted it to my son; I thought he would find it interesting that somebody at Trinity was looking at it. He asked if I read any of it. I said, "No. I'm busy researching Herod." He said I ought to read it because it has a section on Herod. "I might," I said. I thought the section looked fairly small, and I already had books that were entirely devoted to Herod. However, not wanting to disappoint my son, I set aside my pride and read the few pages devoted to Herod. And there it was. I found it! I found the key to understanding Herod; I found the key to understanding myself.

The second paragraph of White's chapter on Herod says the following: "Not long after, in 44 BCE, Antipater's political patron, Julius Caesar, was assassinated in Rome; Antipater himself was soon assassinated by Hasmonean partisans. With Cleopatra's help, Herod fled to Rome and asked Mark Antony and the young Octavian for assistance in reclaiming his father's legacy" (23). This was information I already knew, but at this moment, I knew it in a new way. Herod was an orphan! He was almost thirty-years-old when his father died, and he was already a governor, but he was an orphan nonetheless. His sense of place and security was rocked by his father's assassination. The death of our parents turns us into orphans—no matter our age—but it was more than that for Herod. Herod had to scramble to preserve his own life and his rule.

The lights went on for me in a new way. I had only recently begun to grasp the distinction Paul draws in Galatians 4:4-7 and Romans 8:12-17 between *orphans* and *heirs* (or *slaves* and *sons*). I made this discovery five years after my own Herodian crash; I discovered that both Herod and I likely crashed because of the same issue—we were engaging in what might be called "orphaned behavior." Orphans act in ways that show they have no real sense of home. They have to work *for* home rather than work *from* home. I could see this in Herod's maneuvering, grandiosity, and brutality. I'd already begun to see these behaviors in myself.

First of all, I was not a biological orphan. I am one of five children. My parents put all five of us through college. They raised us to practice solid values of hard work, honesty, lifelong learning, and care for the underserved. They also raised us as Christians. My father lived to be eighty-two, and my mother lived to be almost seventy-nine—long into my adulthood. However, there are ways to be orphaned other than simply growing up without parents. My own "orphanhood" had little to do with my parents. It had to do with my own sense of not belonging—of not measuring up. As one of five children, I often felt that I had to compete for attention and for a place in the family. I tried to earn my spot in the family.

I tried athletics; my father played football in high school and college, so I gave that a try. I was raised in Texas, after all, and back then, almost every boy was to some extent required to try out for football. As a high school freshman, I found out that slow and small is a bad combination for a wannabe wide receiver. One day I caught a pass in practice and a much larger linebacker chased me down and crushed me. I had to be carted off the field on a stretcher. I kept saying, "I'm okay! I'm okay!" Nothing was broken; but I was not okay. I was an orphan; I played football more for my father and schoolmates than for my own enjoyment. Tennis was a much better match (pun unintended), and I was decent enough to play in college at what today is called the Division III level. However, not even being good enough to play on a Division I team fueled my feelings of orphanness in my athletic career.

I also tried academics. With three academic degrees under my belt, I can assure you that more education does not equal less orphaned behavior. My pastor in my college years, Harold Goodenough, used to brag about my good grades, the fact that I earned them while playing tennis, and that it only took me three years to graduate where it took most others four. He was encouraging. He even raised some money in the church to help me pay for books while I was in seminary. He would be surprised to know that my academic achievement turned out to be more of a measure of how far I was *from* Jesus than how close I was *to* Jesus. He might not know that I really was not at home in the faith during college because I was busy trying to earn what can only be received.

In many ways, I think of myself as the older Private Ryan returning to Normandy and the grave of Captain Miller. Years earlier, while dying from the wounds he received in his effort to save Private Ryan, Captain Miller told Ryan that he had "better be worth the effort." Miller told Ryan to go home and cure a disease or make a longer lasting light bulb—to do something worthwhile and meaningful. Years later at the Allied cemetery, the elderly Private Ryan said to his wife, "Tell me I was worth it. Tell me I am a good man."

I tried and competed in many areas of my life in attempt to find a sense of home and acceptance. I even tried ordained ministry for this task. I remember thinking, "Everybody likes pastors. Right?" I do not want to downplay at all that God has indeed called me into ordained ministry, but I wonder if God used my orphaned heart to cement that call in me. My orphaned heart may have gotten me into ordained ministry, but it simply could not sustain me there. My need to gain approval and a sense of place from my congregation members and my fellow church leaders clearly contributed to my crash in 2004.

I can see now that God was trying to show me I was not an orphan all along. I recall reading a book early on in my ministry by John R. Claypool called *Opening Blind Eyes*. Claypool was raised in Texas by parents who believed in him and told him that one day he would be somebody, but he interpreted that to mean that he was not somebody until he became somebody later in life. His book follows his journey to becoming somebody. Like me, he pursued the routes of academic excellence and pastoral ministry. He graduated from Baylor University and went to divinity school at Yale. In spite of these achievements, he did not feel that he was somebody yet. He completed a doctorate at the Southern Baptist seminary in Louisville, Kentucky. He also became the pastor of a five thousand-member Baptist church, but he still lacked the feeling of "being somebody" that he desperately wanted.

Claypool confessed his feelings of what I would call "orphanhood" to his colleague—an Episcopal priest. This priest asked Claypool if he believed in the truth of the Bible. Of course he did; he is a Southern Baptist! The priest then pointed out Matthew 5:13: Jesus says, "You are the light of the world," not, "you might be" or, "you could be if you did certain things." He noted that the verse is in the indicative mode—"you are." It was as if scales fell from Claypool's eyes and they were opened to the fact that he did not have to *become* somebody. He *already was* somebody! For Claypool, the experience called to mind psychologist Sam Keen's citing of a Buddhist proverb: most of us are like a man riding on an ox and yet looking for an ox. What we seek so desperately is right there with us all the time. My eyes were also opened—partially. Like the blind man of Mark 8:22, I would need a second touch. Mine was a long, long, journey from orphan to heir.

In general, what are orphans like? How are they different from heirs? In general, orphans have to secure their own a place in a home. Paul also uses the term "slave." Because they work *for* the home and the family, they are at risk of losing their place *in* the home and the family. Servants or slaves, therefore, live in a state of fear and anxiety. They cannot trust that life will work out for them in the family the way a son or daughter can trust that it will. Thus, they try to arrange their lives in a way that provides security. This behavior was clearly evident in Herod. When his father died and his people were, in many ways, rebelling, he went to Antony for security—for a home place. He became "more

Roman than the Romans." He adopted the Roman Hellenistic culture and became one of Hellenism's primary propagators in that part of the world. His befriending of Mark Antony and, later, Octavian (Augustus Caesar) seemed to be Herod's attempt at being adopted into the Roman family and culture. His travel itineraries illustrate the fact that he did not have a secure family standing. When he escaped rebellion in Judea, he immediately sailed for Rome, where he was named "King of the Jews." As previously noted, his palaces formed an escape route, by which he could go from the Mediterranean Sea to the Dead Sea and escape his enemies. Herod was a king, and yet, he was a man without a country or family.

I can see the orphan behavior in my own life as well. For me, this need for place came out in my attempt to impress other people (specifically my congregants and those in church leadership with me). Perhaps they would grant me the identity as a member of their family; maybe they could provide me with a sense of home and security. But, as you might have guessed, this did not work out. First, I simply could not please everyone all the time. When I looked to others for security, I placed my fate in the hands of people who are very different from one another and from me. What pleases one person will not please another. We, church leaders and pastors, tend to learn this lesson the hard way. We try to keep everyone happy and realize eventually that this activity is tiringly impossible.

Fred Craddock tells a story about a pastor who came to a new church. The church had a barbecue for him on his very first Sunday. At the barbecue, he asked the head of the search committee what the congregation's vote looked like in naming him the church's new pastor. The man told the pastor it was almost unanimous. "What do you mean 'almost unanimous'?" the new pastor asked. "What was the exact count?" The man replied, "Almost unanimous; it was seventy for and three against." The pastor spent the next six months finding out who those three people who voted against him were; he then did everything he could to curry their favor. Unfortunately, those efforts took him away from pastoral tasks that needed his attention. The church voted to let him go a year later. And can you guess what the vote was? Seventy for firing him and three against! Almost any action you take as a pastor will be opposed by someone, and if that action is calling for a significant change, even a positive change, it will be opposed by many.

I cannot help but think of the people in Mark chapter 5 who preferred to see the demoniac naked and bloody as opposed to dressed and "in his right mind." I remember how stunned I was to learn that even improvements I introduced to congregations were opposed. How can anyone object to new carpet that did not cost the church a penny? Well, it was not the right color...even though it was the same color as the carpet we were replacing! People are fickle. Have you ever noticed that a person can be pleased with you at one moment and upset with you the next? We even see this fickle nature in our spouses! As my friend once said, the plain truth of the matter is this: "The people I am trying so desperately to please are as messed up as I am."

Though I should know better theologically, I took the same approach with God. I tried to find ways to impress the Father. I am like my cat who brings dead lizards to my backdoor; I want to show God my work. I have taken so many things to God's backdoor: sermons, times of prayer, acts of service to others, practices of spiritual disciplines, etc. I seem to be unconsciously asking God to tell me I'm a good man. "Tell me I am worth dying for." The problems with this approach are numerous. It shows a complete misunderstanding of grace and the nature of God. There are practical issues with it as well. How does one impress the creator of the universe? Does God point out the wonders of a planet, an ocean full of unique creatures, a waterfall in the Rockies, and then add, "Oh, and did y'all hear David's sermon last week? Amazing!" There is no lizard out there big and bad enough to bring to heaven's back porch. I had to ask myself, when have you done enough to earn grace from the one who moved heaven and Earth to save you? What can you give in exchange for your soul? Under the glow of God's grace and greatness, nothing is big enough, and no amount of effort is sufficient to offer. Thankfully, God is not waiting for us to impress him with our abilities or works—but we will get to that soon enough.

How, then, do sons and daughters act? How do heirs behave? Heirs clearly behave differently than orphans do. They know they have a home. They stand to inherit from the family; they do not have to secure payment or reward from the family. Heirs act in ways that are less anxious and fearful. They tend not to be manipulative like orphans are. They have the ability to *receive* life because they are not as busy trying to *arrange* life.

Taking from the works of Mark Stibbe, I have a list of possible signs that would indicate that I am behaving in an orphaned manner rather than in the manner of an heir. I caution you: this list is much more helpful as a mirror turned inward on ourselves and not as a lens through which to label or judge others.

1. Mistrust: When I doubt the motives of people around me, I often discover that this doubt says more about me than it does about other people. Herod suffered from extreme mistrust. Unfortunately, his mistrust was lethal to those around him, including his sons, his favorite wife, and many seemingly innocent peasants.

2. Hiding: When I attempt to hide or withdraw from others, it is often due to my habit of acting out of fear that I will not be accepted for my true self. I fear that I will lose my place or home. I've fallen prey to what Nelson Mandela referred to as "playing small." Mandela reminded us that playing small does not help anyone. When I refuse to act or speak out in a difficult situation, it is often more a function of fear than of prudence (though the Scriptures wisely counsel us to watch our tongues). Herod literally hid in his palace fortresses. Hiding can also be due to my unwillingness to admit or display my vulnerability to other people. I can hide in broad daylight by not letting myself be vulnerable with others in my pain or fear. Herod certainly hid his vulnerability behind the shield of intimidation, power, consumption, and ruthless brutality.

3. Superficiality: My superficiality is intimately connected to my hiding. When I do not live out of my deep acceptance as a "son," I will not willingly dig deeply into my life or be with other people while they dig into theirs. Only when I'm convinced that I am "safe" will I take the risk of living deeply and truthfully with others and myself. I cannot attempt to assess Herod's level of superficiality. That would involve significant projection on my part, and projection is another sign of orphaned behavior! However, Herod certainly exhibits a sense of grandiosity, which makes me wonder if his concern over palaces, harbors, temples, and other external matters allowed him to disregard more internal matters.

4. Manipulation: I heard Henry Cloud say, "Control is the curse of all human relationships." Control also is a sign that my relationship with God, others, and myself is out of alignment. When I'm feeling orphaned, I will look for any means to secure my place in the present and the future. Rather than live fully in the present moment, I will look for ways to move others and myself into positions that will be favorable to my future. This attempt to take control directly opposes my sense of what life lived as an heir looks like; the life of an heir looks like children playing freely and happily among many swings and toys in a large, secure, fenced-in yard. Manipulation (orphanhood) looks more like a slow, bitter game of chess between two rivals. As an orphan, I try to get ahead; I miss the joy of the moment.

Herod engaged in manipulation in many ways: He manipulated his family through violence and in the writing of at least six different versions of his final will and testament. He manipulated the Romans through his alliances and his gifts of temples and tribute to the Emperor. Finally, he tried to manipulate the masses through his massive employment program and temple project while forcing employees to live under the threat of brutality and revenge.

5. Anger: I went through an exercise recently that made me realize that anger is one of the dominant negative emotions I experience with my congregation. My anger is not explosive; it is not always even apparent to the majority of congregants. It is more like Henri Nouwen's "frozen anger"—a passive aggressiveness that causes me to disengage from people whom I see as not being "enough" (*The Way of the Heart*, 24). I fill in the blank with those I see as committed, generous, caring, and grateful people. Using this strategy, I can write off people as unworthy and release myself from the responsibility of maintaining relationships with them. Not surprisingly, the amount of anger I feel (which I also experience as sadness) is related to the insecurity I have about myself. The more insecure I feel, the more likely I am to engage in passive aggressive ways. Insecurity and the resulting anger are major warning lights on my spiritual dashboard telling me I'm indulging my orphan fantasies and ignoring the truth about my status in God's family. With his acts of murder and revenge, Herod's anger is much more obvious than mine. Friend and foe alike felt the wrath of his orphaned heart.

6. *Competition*: Pastors and church leaders are often a competitive lot. We find ways to mention our victories in somber, humble tones. We mention we are having trouble getting more than five thousand people to participate in our month-long prayer and fasting experience; we say we are having difficulties with one of our children and that this painful episode made us decide to turn down the offer to

be the keynote speaker at the White House prayer breakfast. For years, anytime I would enter a room of church leaders, I would immediately begin to size up the competition to see where I was on the ecclesial pecking order: "Oh, he has twenty-five services each weekend." "She has already published three books." "His church just tried to get rid of him!" This behavior is never a sign of good health. My friends and family will tell you that I am naturally a competitive person. Our health insurance company recently required us to wear a pedometer as part of a wellness program. I wear mine from the time I get up in the morning until I go to bed at night, and each week I proudly tell my wife that I walk more than ninety-five percent of the people in my organization. I read about the early Methodist circuit riders who risked life and limb to carry the gospel to the frontier, and I wonder how many steps I could get credit for if I traveled from the East Coast to Tennessee! That competitive spirit may help me walk for my physical health, but it can do only harm to my spiritual health. Orphans need to compete—to prove that they are worthy of a place in the household. Herod was an Olympic athlete who wanted to be known as the greatest architect and builder in history. He also wanted to be seen as the most generous benefactor and patron in the Roman world. He was definitely a competition-driven orphan.

7. Drivenness: When I behave as a driven person more than a called person, my orphaned heart is in full gear and has the pedal to the floor. When I cannot rest from labor, take joy in my small victories, or spend time with loved ones because there's so much still to do for God, it is not because I am a saint. It is because I'm living out of my sin. Drivenness can come disguised as a passion for God and for God's mission, but it is really a result of a lack of trust in God. When my should-do's and ought-to's outnumber my get to's, I know my heart is on the wrong track. I was well aware of the dangers of drivenness by my arrival at AHUMC in 1995 when I first read Gordon MacDonald's book, *Ordering Your Private World*. However, I learned over time that no amount of vigilance can keep me from acting driven if I do not have a sense of acceptance and belonging in my life—if I do not feel at home. It may seem like competitiveness and drivenness are very similar concepts, and they are in my life. They are symptomatic not of a passion for God as many on the outside may believe but of an undervalued sense of God's passion for us as God's children. Herod certainly looks driven to me. He could never rest—not even when he was swimming in money, fame, power, and architectural accomplishments. True rest never comes from external sources; it comes from what God does in our internal selves.

Perhaps we should take a timeout here. It is time for a reality check. The fact of the matter is that orphaned behavior is socially acceptable in every way and can be effective in *driving* people to achieve goals and status. Required texts from my son's classes come in handy again here: One day he was reading Jon Meacham's classic book on Andrew Jackson, *American Lion*. He read, "Perhaps partly because he was fatherless, [Jackson] may have felt he had to do more than usual to prove his strength and thus secure, or try to secure, his place in the community" (10). I am grateful to Meacham, a respected recipient of the Pulitzer Prize, for helping to make my case here that orphans are trying to secure a place in the world. However, in fairness, we should note that Andrew Jackson, his dealings with the Native Americans aside, was an extremely effective and important leader in American history.

His success probably stemmed from the fact that Jackson was fatherless and therefore lived his life with a consuming desire to prove himself to perceived enemies and friends alike. A quick glance through a history book can show that orphans have often been effective in achieving success and greatness in our world: Alexander the Great, Julius Caesar, Napoleon Bonaparte, George Washington, Queen Victoria, etc. But before we get too excited about that list, we should also remember that Adolf Hitler, Vladimir Lenin, and Joseph Stalin were orphans too. It seems that orphanhood can be leveraged to achieve a number of things—good and evil. However, my own experience of acting out of an orphaned heart shows that even when good is achieved, there are often terrible consequences. Perhaps that is because our God does not call on us to avoid achievement but, rather, calls us to achieve in his Spirit, in his power, and in his will. An orphan is chiefly concerned about his own will and plans as he drives toward his place in the world. We can draw some conclusions about orphan behavior from history and from psychology, but it's also a good idea to see what the Bible has to say about it.

Take for example Luke chapter 15. We have observed the tendency of our Western world to find truth in fact and propositions, but the Eastern world often finds truth in story. A look at one of the most famous of Jesus' stories gives us a better idea of the truth about orphaned behavior. The older brother in the parable of the prodigal son (which would perhaps be better named, "the parable of the loving father") remains at home, but he clearly does not feel that he has a home. He shows a few telltale signs of an orphaned heart. When he heard about the party for the "prodigal" son, the eldest son "became angry and refused to join" (V. 28). Here we see *anger* and *hiddenness*. He tells his father, "You never even gave me a goat" (V. 29). He shows his mistrust of a very trustworthy father and his competitive relationship with his brother. "This son of yours...has squandered your property with prostitutes," he argues (V. 30). This judgment of the way his brother spent his inheritance could be an attempt to manipulate the father's will through projection and blaming. Then, one of the saddest parts of the older brother's behavior is revealed: "My son…Everything I have is yours" (V. 31). The older brother did not lose anything; his inheritance was intact.

The most troubling part of this story is that the older brother completely misreads and misunderstands his father's heart. He misses his father's love and misinterprets the father's love for the younger son as a lack of love for him. He traded his place in the house as a *son* for that of the *servant*. That is never a good trade, but it is one that too many of our church leaders make. We trade our unconditional acceptance as children for a life of slaving away in the kingdom, hoping somehow to earn a place at the father's table. Bill Hume hit it right on the head when he said, "It is easier to believe that God exists than to believe that God loves us!" Yes, the journey from orphan to heir is a long and a more difficult one than we might imagine, but it can be taken. I took the journey, and everything changed.

CHAPTER FIVE

Living as an Heir

~

We have heard it said that the longest journey we ever take is from the head to the heart. That is certainly true of my journey from orphan to a son and an heir in God's house. Back in 1983, John Claypool planted the seed of "sonship" in my head. In 1984, I participated in a retreat called The Walk to Emmaus. My experience that weekend further taught me that I was a child in the family of God. Henri Nouwen's writings about being the beloved and having a home provided even more support for the idea of sonship. Brennan Manning's books, *The Ragamuffin Gospel* and *Abba's Child*, in the decade following moved me further in the direction of living out of my acceptance by a loving father. I knew theologically that I was an heir, but that knowledge did not affect the way I was living. It had not moved into my heart. I needed another touch to see clearly.

The second touch came in a profound way in 2006. Our church was hosting a spiritual life conference, and I signed up for a seminar led by a pastor from South Africa named Trevor Hudson. I heard good things about his ministry, and I went to the seminar eager to hear him speak. In a seminar on avoiding burnout (an important topic for me since the event of my Herodian crash two years earlier), he mentioned the work of Dr. Frank Lake in a 1966 book, *Clinical Theology*. In this book, Lake introduced a concept called the "dynamic cycle of being." This cycle divides life into input and output. He applied this cycle to Jesus and found that Jesus began his ministry with the input of unconditional acceptance from the Father. Jesus heard the voice at his baptism say, "You are my son. I love you. You bring me happiness" (Mark 1:8). Jesus then added to that the additional input of sustenance—the activities that fed Jesus' soul, such as the study of Scripture, fellowship, and prayer. On the output side, Lake said that Jesus' own being—his presence—carried significance. Hudson noted that Jesus could change a room without saying or doing anything. He affected change simply by being. Lake called the final output "achievement." This included the various ministerial acts of Jesus with which we are familiar: preaching, teaching, healing, and performing other miracles. Hudson preferred the word "fruitfulness" to "achievement" and termed this "a cycle of grace."

In his seminar, Hudson told us that we, church leaders, burn out because we start on the wrong side of that cycle. We start with our ministry works (achievements and fruitfulness) and work backward in attempt to gain acceptance. We tend to minister *for* acceptance rather than *from* acceptance. Not only is this dangerously wrong theologically, but it inevitably leads to pain and disappointment. Hudson called this a "cycle of works." Two things struck me as I sat in the seminar room that afternoon. First, it struck me that I had been doing ministry backwards. I had been trying to perform in attempt to gain acceptance rather than ministering out of acceptance. Secondly, I realized that the more I live out of acceptance and sustenance, the more likely it is that my actual presence and being will become a positive influence on other people. Hudson said, "We will never give ourselves away in ministry until we know ourselves as God's Beloved." I left that day one giant step closer to knowing myself as God's beloved.

Unfortunately, unlike the blind man in Mark chapter 8, I would require a third touch to make this journey of identity. My third touch came in 2008 when my identity as the beloved began to reach the outer regions of my heart. It started when one of my younger colleagues, Scott, began to show up on time for our meetings. This punctuality was unusual for him; he was passionate, extroverted, and energetic, and he was always on the phone, always finishing a conversation, and always coming up with a new idea. He often took phone calls during our meetings. Some people saw his behavior as disrespectful; I thought it was his youthful exuberance, though this exuberance had been going on for ten years. Then, suddenly, Scott began to show up on time for our meetings and putting his phone away for their duration. He apologized for not honoring me and for following his own sense of God's plan when he was on our main campus more than supporting my view of God's plan. He apologized for the trouble he had caused me by overstepping the boundaries our finance committee gave him when he started Riverside. He asked for a chance to address the staff and more publically apologize for not supporting me in my role as senior pastor. He also wanted to speak at a Sunday morning worship service. He made all those public apologies to an amazed and confused staff and congregation; they were confused because they, and I, thought pastors and laypeople alike were supposed to follow their own interpretations of God's plan.

He had my attention. I was intrigued. "Okay, what is up?" I asked. He explained his view of sonship. His friend Mel had recently shared some lectures on the subject by a man named Jack Frost (yes...that is his real name). The lectures were called "From Slavery to Sonship." Scott walked me through passages like Romans 8:14-17 and Galatians 4:1-7, which say that in Christ we are children of God and are therefore heirs to a wonderful inheritance. We do not have to work for our place in God's house. It is given to us. At that time, he was not telling me anything that I did not already know; but, of course, the knowledge was stuck only in my head. As we talked and as I listened to the recordings, which were not easy to listen to, as the speaker had some interesting mannerisms and was not a seminary-trained theologian, I began to relearn some critical things. As I further researched the subject, I learned again that life as an heir involves working *from* approval not *for* approval. I learned again that my identity as an heir consists chiefly in belovedness and acceptance. I learned that our work is done not *for* rest but *from* rest. I learned a completely different way of being. I no longer had to strive to make my place in God's house and in the world;

I already had a place there! The most important piece of my life is something that I cannot earn; it is something I can only receive.

As I continued to research the subject, especially through the writings of Dr. Mark Stibbe, I began to learn that this way of living and being had deep theological roots. Stibbe helped me see that this concept of sonship has a rich history in the church as the theological doctrine of adoption. Using the metaphor of Luke chapter 15, Stibbe calls adoption the lost coin of our Christian theology. He should say that it is the lost *side* of the coin; he goes on to point out that adoption and justification by faith are two sides of the same theological coin. They were, at one time, the two main theological pillars of the Christian faith, but the adoption side of the coin was lost as we "focused on the finished work on the cross (justification) but not the continuing work of the Spirit (adoption)" (*From Orphans to Heirs: Bible Reading Fellowship*, 13). The theology of adoption can be traced through the Hebrew Bible as God transforms the people from slavery in Egypt to inheritors of the Promised Land. Paul talks about adoption in Romans chapter 8 and Galatians chapter 4. Stibbe notes that in the Roman world, three things happened when a slave was adopted by his master: first, the slave became free; second, the slave became an heir in the new family; and third, all the slave's debts were canceled. Paul, no doubt, saw the rich tie between the Roman practice of adoption and the gifts that are given to us through our own adoption in Christ. In John 14:8, Jesus promised his followers, "I will not leave you orphans."

The early church noticed this biblical theme. Origen believed that the goal of the gospel was to bring the believer into a father-son relationship with the living God. John Wesley, the father of Methodism, spoke often of the "loving spirit of adoption." Between 1739 and 1743, Wesley preached on Romans 8:15 at least fourteen times out of his desire to see people enter into sonship: “The Spirit you received does not make you slaves so that you live in fear again; rather, the spirit you received brought about your adoption to sonship. And by him we cry, Abba, Father" (Romans 8:15). In the description of his May 24, 1738 conversion, in which he speaks of his heart being "strangely warmed," Wesley writes of an end to his striving. He moved from slave to son—from orphan to heir.

Charles Spurgeon, the great nineteenth century expositor, also highlighted adoption. Spurgeon wrote, "If you want to judge how well a person understands Christianity, first find out how much he makes of the thought of being God's child and having God as his father" (Quoted in Stibbe, *From Orphans to Heirs*, 115) Though it is clear to me that adoption took a backseat in the theological car to justification by faith in the church's theology after the Reformation, it was not simply thrown out the window! Lake, Claypool, Nouwen, Manning, and others clearly found adoption foundational to their ideas about faith.

This rediscovery of adoption proved to be a happy event for me in my life as a beloved disciple and also as a pastor. It helped me see the concept of “being like Christ” in a new light. While I remain convinced that Dallas Willard is correct in saying we do not become like Jesus because we do not engage in the spiritual practices in which he engaged (such as prayer, worship, Scripture, community, service, and solitude), I also see that Lake is right that the first input is acceptance, not these activities of sustenance. In other words, if I want to be more like Jesus, my starting point cannot be to focus on Jesus and his activities but to put my focus where Jesus put his own focus: on being a beloved child of the Father. In the words of Jack Frost, "Jesus was busy being a son" (*Spiritual Slavery to Spiritual Sonship*, 157). I understand why we, as

Christians, are sometimes a little slow to become more missional in our hearts and hands; we put so much emphasis on being saved (justification) that there does not appear to be much of a reason to be on the planet after "salvation." However, as an adopted child, I am motivated to work in the family business and do what the Father is doing (more on that in chapter 6).

But even after all this, it seemed that my identity as a child and heir had not yet made it to the deepest part of my heart. When Scott shared the "S" word (submission) with me, my identity began to sink in. He talked about the biblical concept of submission. It was not an attractive word to me. I remember preaching years ago at a wedding on Ephesians 5:21-33; when I read "submit to one another" and "submit to your husband," the bride's bouquet started twitching. I thought she was going to hit me with it! I couldn't blame her. Submission has been given a bad name in certain political, social, and socioeconomic issues (e.g., gender relations), specifically among Christians.

Submission seems to indicate a groveling and subservient stance in life. It seems to support the oppression of certain kinds of people by other kinds of people. But Scott quickly corrected my misunderstanding; he stressed that the biblical picture of submission is one of bending low in order to lift up. We bow down not to stay down and grovel but to honor and support another. Children submits to parents by not only subservience but also by doing what they can to help their parents accomplish plans and reach goals. Scott was teaching me about the missing link in my journey: we cannot live as a child of God unless we live as a child of our own biological and spiritual parents. I cannot know myself as a son to God if I do not live as a son to those whom God has placed over me.

I have heard countless messages and read book after book about my identity as a beloved child, but I always lived as an independent and free agent. It is no wonder I could not experience the transition Stibbe called moving from "objective reality to subjective reality." One day I found a beautiful picture of this at the library. I was thumbing through a book by David Flusser, a Jewish scholar, called *Judaism of the Second Temple Period.* In the forward to the book, his student, David Bivins, wrote about his efforts to get this German book translated to and published in English: "In my judgment, disciples should assure that all the unpublished material of a prominent teacher is published before they publish their own research. The teacher's work takes precedence over the disciple's." Written from the perspective of a rabbi-disciple relationship, this quote is a perfect illustration of how submission should work. It is a joyful offering—not a grudging obligation. John the Baptist understood submission well in his relationship with Jesus: "He must become greater; I must become less" (John 3:30).

My mind and heart had now come together to embrace my newly discovered identity, and I set out to become the best son I could be to my earthly father. I was never a bad son; I didn't really have much of a teenage rebellion period. But as an adult, I was clearly living for my own life and did not care much about my dad's life. He was aging and caring fulltime for my mother, who had Alzheimer's. They lived three hours away from me, so I would usually just call them on Sunday nights. To practice my sonship submission, I told myself that I would drive down at least once a month to spend part of the day with my dad. I would drop my son off at school, drive down, spend a few hours over lunch with dad, and then drive back in time to pick up my son from practice. This plan worked well for a few months. Then I hit some bumps: a funeral here, son's tennis tournament there. Soon, I had missed three straight months except for trips home at Thanksgiving and on Christmas Day.

Then, on New Year's Day 2009, I called home and Mom answered. That was unusual because Dad usually answered the phone so we would not hear how bad my mom was getting. "Where is Dad?" I asked. "He's in the bathtub and can't get out," she said. Fortunately, my older brother lived near them, so he helped Dad. He found out that Dad had the flu and Mom was in need of hospitalization for her disease. I did not miss my visit that month. We children had our hands full. The next month, my older brother died suddenly from a stroke. After his funeral, we convinced my parents to move to San Antonio where my younger brother and I live. I spent time with my dad three days of every week for the next three and a half years until his death. I was blessed with the privilege of being a son, even though some of the duties I performed were not enjoyable. I knew that I was growing as a son in the faith while I experienced my earthly father's love in new ways. Dad always thanked me for everything I did for him, and he never forgot to tell me he loved me.

I, and my colleagues, had other earthly fathers to submit to as well. We had to come a long way from our orphan days. Scott, Michael, and I flew a pirate flag on the back wall of my office for many years. It was our way of saying we were not interested in being the "flagship" of our denomination as a large church; we wanted to chart our own course. Yes, we were all orphans at that time! In the wake of this change to our understanding of sonship, Scott and I set out to lift up our bishop and district superintendent; we wanted to let them know that we were here to serve them. We met with Bishop Dorff and offered to support him in any way he needed. He was gracious and responded that he wanted to serve us. We explained that we understood that God had placed us here to serve his, the bishop's, mission. I also told our superintendent, Carl Rohlfs, that I would do whatever he asked me to do (as long as it was not immoral, un-biblical, or illegal...of course).

This submission has not been without sacrifice. When the bishop asked me to be on a task force that met two days every month (not counting conference calls) I swallowed hard and accepted. When I was in the introductory meeting for the task force and we were asked to share why we were there, I told them I was there because the bishop asked me to be there—not because of any particular contribution I thought I could make. The other members were confused by that response. The commitment to the task force was not an easy one—especially since I'm not a fan of meetings. Looking back, I can see that I received the blessing of forming many new relationships on that task force and of playing a small role in an important undertaking in our judicatory when the task force worked to unite our Southwest Texas Annual Conference with the Rio Grande Conference of the United Methodist Church.

Stemming from our desire to honor our earthly spiritual authority figures, a group of people from our church now meets with the superintendent and the denominational officer in charge of church planting for our conference on a regular basis to pray for and with them. Our submission, again, it is not about groveling; it is about honoring. It is not about promoting ourselves; it is about promoting what our spiritual parents are doing.

My original fear was that this emphasis on submission could lead to oppression and spiritual abuse on the part of authorities. Quite the opposite has been true; as I have sought to honor my parents, biological and spiritual, I have found them eager to bless me as well. As

I live as a son to spiritual fathers, which for me also includes some key lay mentors in my church, the "subjective reality" of my identity continues to grow more permanent. Additionally, I am amazed that, as I have lived more faithfully as a son, I have actually been given many opportunities to father others. I have many "children"; many more people than ever before are devoted to lifting me up and to helping me accomplish the mission the Father has given me. Years ago, I read in Nouwen's book *Return of the Prodigal* that there comes a time when sons must become fathers. He noted that, at times, we have been the wandering younger brother and, at other times, we have been the dutiful older brother, but there comes a time to be the father. That has become a joyous reality for me. I might add to Nouwen's thought that we can only be spiritual fathers if we have *first* been sons.

KEYS TO EXPERIENCING OUR IDENTITY

Submission was key to my ability to move from objective reality as an orphan to subjective reality as an heir. However, my reading of Mark Stibbe and Jack Frost, along with my experience of leading others on this identity journey, reveals several more things that are helpful for experiencing the reality of our identity as children of the loving Father:

Change to my image of God: It is helpful to revise our image and our understanding of God. We need to see God more as Father—not just the king of the universe. Mel Schwartz, who introduced the concept of identity to our Alamo Heights family of churches, observed that it is easier to move from the image of God as Father to God as King then it is to move from the image of God as King (and judge) to God as Father. One of the downsides to our heavy Protestant emphasis on justification is that it leaves us with the dominant image of God as judge and bookkeeper. Stibbe mentions the famous photo of President John F. Kennedy and his son "John John" in the oval office; the child is playing contentedly under his father's desk while his father is on the phone. John John does not know the power and influence that his father has in his role as President; he is only aware of how his loving father cares for him. I have no doubt in God's ability to rule the universe, but I do have doubts as to whether we can live into our identity as children if we do not adequately focus on the love of God as Father. Jesus models this understanding in his own communication with God as "Abba" and in the communication model he gave to us—the Lord's Prayer—in which he teaching us to address God as "Our Father."

There are many people who have had dysfunctional, possibly abusive, earthly fathers and therefore find the "God the father" image troubling and painful. I am aided by the wisdom of James Bryan Smith, who notes that we have it backwards when we measure our heavenly Father by the image of our earthly fathers. It should be the other way around. We should instead allow God to redefine who we aim to be as earthly parents.

Face the pain of the past: It is important for me to face the pain I have endured from my experience of rejection. In truth, I drew conclusions about life and about my identity from that rejection that were not true. I shared with the church a silly experience from early childhood that caused pain and caused me to withdraw and hide as an adult. When I was in the third grade, my teacher left the room briefly. A girl stood up and offered free candy bars to the class. We all got in line for the unexpected prize. I was, unfortunately, last in that long line and the teacher walked in when I was the only one still left standing because I had not yet received my candy. My teacher informed me that she would have to tell my mother, who was also a teacher in the school, about the incident. My teacher told me I should know better. I was embarrassed and ashamed. Though I can see now that it is natural for a young boy to want candy and that my teacher was only seeking order in the classroom, I drew the conclusion that I was an embarrassment and it would be better for me to lay low in life than to be exposed for the embarrassment I really was. I adopted a way of life that "protected me." I played small and tried to remain unnoticed unless I was certain I was right. I failed to trust the intentions of authority figures, including my own parents, and drew unfair conclusions about them. I was also convinced that I was not valuable and gifted. With the help of friends in a process called Faithwalking, I have recently begun to articulate this pain and have come to a realization of how God really feels about me (more about Faithwalking in chapter 7). "What is unshared is unhealed"; as I brought my pain and perceived rejection into the open, I have begun to live more deeply into my identity as a child of the loving Father.

Repent of orphan tendencies: I've learned the need to recognize and repent of the orphan tendencies (chapter 4) in my life. There are a number of telltale signs that I am acting with orphan tendencies. A helpful saying for me is, "What does not get *talked* out gets *acted* out." When I recognize orphaned behavior in my life, I confess it to the people

I trust. I repent of it before a loving Father and invite my trusted friends to hold me accountable. For example, if I find myself trying to impress other people by putting on a front that shows me to be more than I am, I recognize that I am not living fully into all that God believes about me. I confess this to friends, they receive the confession, and they let me know that I am valuable to God. I often have to confess that I need the approval of others and that I fear rejection; these needs and fears often cause me hold back on truthful speech or necessary vulnerability.

Forgive my fathers: It is also important to forgive my earthly father and other authority figures for the pain I experienced. I am well aware that it was often *my perception* of an authority figure's action and not the action itself that caused the pain; however, our earthly fathers and mothers are not perfect. We must forgive them for their failings. Forgiveness frees us to do a better job of submitting to and honoring their authority. We can even offer forgiveness and honor to our authority figures after their earthly death. I speak well of my parents every chance I get. I was able to forgive my father of any mistakes he made and seek his forgiveness for the ways I did not submit to and honor him before he died. I'm so fortunate that my father spent his last few years living just a few miles away from me. Stibbe wrote, "God will not do a great work through us until God has done a great work in us" (*I Am Your Father*, 307). I'm sure he is right. Practicing and living in forgiveness with my parents opened up wonderful conversations with parishioners about their own family relationships.

Experience the Father's Embrace: It is also important to experience the Father's embrace personally. I borrow that phrase from Jack Frost. I need to experience the Father's love for me personally. A powerful way I experience God's love is in groups of trusted people who love me unconditionally. I can share my orphan tendencies of manipulation, hiding, or fear; they respond with love and acceptance and call me to a higher level of living as an heir. I can picture myself sitting like a small child in the lap of my heavenly Father. I can curl up in complete security and rest. I also picture my Father walking beside me and holding with my hand in His through previously uncharted territory.

Turn off my shame voice: I truly cannot live as a son while allowing the voice of shame to speak to me. I believe we all have an inner voice of shame that tries to convince us we are not worthy, we are not valuable, and we are alone in the world. This voice is quick to jump in and magnify my mistakes; it says, "See? I told you that you couldn't do it." When I have unhealthy thoughts, it chimes in: "If people only knew how angry you are, they would never listen to a word you say from the pulpit." While I write this book, my shame is whispering, "Why would anyone want to read this?" Maybe you believe my shame voice is a prophetic utterance from the Lord, but I believe it is the voice of the Evil One, whom Jesus so accurately labeled "the accuser." Trusted people help me here as well. I have learned to "out" the shame voice by speaking it aloud to those who can help me see that it is not the voice of God.

My heir-identity is slowly making its way from my head to the outer regions of my heart and digging its way into the core. It surprised me how this happened; it was not as I cleaned up my act but as I brought to light my issues and their root cause—an orphan identity. What I began to reveal in broken pieces has remarkably become a whole only in my willingness to confess and confront the Herod-like tendencies that were driving my life. This process resembles a parable by Soren Kierkegaard, which I first heard from Fred Craddock:

A new priest came to a small village church that was in need of a new cloth for the altar. The priest made inquiries and found out whom the best seamstress in the church was. He asked her to make the new altar cloth.

"Father, I could never make a cloth beautiful enough for the altar of God," she answered.

He insisted, and she reluctantly agreed. After a few weeks, he asked her how it was going, but she said she was having trouble finding material that was beautiful enough for the altar. He told her to find some and start on it.

A few weeks later, he asked her again how it was going. She begged him to let her start all over again because it was not beautiful enough for the altar of God.

"Finish it and bring it to me!" he told her.

The next week he asked her if the cloth was finished yet. She said it was, but that she did not bring it to him because it just was not right for the altar.

"Go home and get it," the priest insisted. With great reluctance, she brought it to him, but she asked again to start all over.

"Take it out of the bag, and put it on the altar," he ordered. She did so, and as she looked at it on the table, she gasped.

"Why, Father!" she said. "It is more beautiful than I made it!"

"My child, don't you understand?" the priest answered. "That is how God does it. He makes everything beautiful."

As I have dared to unfold the fabric of my orphaned life in the presence of the loving Father, I have experienced the same reality as the seamstress: God has taken my orphaned life and heart and made it more beautiful than I could ever make it by my own efforts. In the words of the musical group Gungor, "You make beautiful things. You make beautiful things out of the dust. You make beautiful things...you make beautiful things out of us."

CHAPTER SIX

The Family Business

~

"Some people are so heavenly minded that they are of no earthly good." Some attribute that quote to Oliver Wendell Holmes. In Mere Christianity, C.S. Lewis makes a famous reply: "If you read history, you will find that the Christians who did most for the present world were just those who thought most of the next…It is since Christians have largely ceased to think of the other world that they have become so ineffective in this. Aim at heaven and you will get Earth thrown in: aim at Earth and you will get neither."

An interesting debate emerges in these famous quotes. I see evidence on both sides. I've seen dedicated Christians talk profusely about stories of heaven while standing idly by as the Earth seems to be going straight to hell in a hand basket; I have also seen people make great sacrifices for the betterment of the Earth while simultaneously anticipating their reward and rest in heaven. I would like to add another possibility: What if we focus not on heaven above or below but, rather, on heaven here on Earth? What if we saw our task as seeing through to completion the task Christ began in his life, death, and resurrection: creating God's kingdom on the Earth as it is in heaven? If we took up this task, we would be joining our father in what N.T. Wright calls "the family business."

It strikes me that adoption theology has a distinct advantage over justification-by-faith in answering this most important question of "Now what?" The forensic emphasis of justification stresses our acquittal and offers few clues as to what else we are to do following acquittal other than hope that we won't behave so poorly again. Paul saw the danger of "double jeopardy"; if we have been acquitted once, are we not free to do more of the same behavior simply because we are now off the hook and will no longer receive our just punishment (Romans 6:1). The family aspect of the adoption theology seems to hint at an answer to the "Now what?" question: You are in the family, so go and act like a family member.

It is likely that Paul's Jewish contemporaries had a better sense of this than we do. They did not have the wide range of vocational choices that we have today. They were expected to go into the family business. If your father was a carpenter (more accurately a 'stonemason'...but we've discussed that before), then you are likely going to become a carpenter. The strong communal aspect of the Ancient Near East placed family needs over the individual's desires. Better stated: the individual desired what was best for the family and supported the family business, whether that business was in making millstones or baskets.

Jesus was clear that the Father's business was His kingdom—the "kingdom of God." Pious Jews would have called it the "kingdom of heaven" in an effort to protect God's name given to Moses in the Exodus account of the burning bush. It does not refer to a place that is separate from Earth—a separate place called "heaven." As we know, Jesus taught more about the kingdom of God than about any other subject. Parables, descriptions, accounts of events, and teachings in each of the gospel accounts point to this recurring theme in Jesus' ministry. Smarter and wiser people than I have written about Jesus and the kingdom. I find helpful N.T. Wright's work in *How God Became King* and *Simply Jesus*. There is a growing awareness in our day that the main message and activity of Jesus had to do with the expansion of the kingdom of God. There are a number of definitions of the kingdom of God circulating, but I find this most helpful: the kingdom of God is "where God's rule is enacted" or "where God's activity is taking place." Jesus indicates in the prayer he gives to his disciples that the kingdom comes when "God's will is done." I think of it as the act of bringing heaven to Earth or making Earth more like heaven.

Over the centuries, we have acted as if Jesus' main message was "believe in me and go to heaven." We've asked, "If you died tonight, do you know where you would go?" It seems to me that Jesus was more about life than death, more about faith than belief, and more about Earth than heaven. It seems to me that our forensic approach to salvation gives us only one place to go following our acquittal: heaven. The family approach we find in adoption theology puts our attention on where the Father is working: Earth. We have limited salvation to a "do this and go to heaven" message, but I think God had so much more in mind. God had individuals and all of creation in mind in God's kingdom efforts. In Romans chapter 8, Paul assures us that all of creation is in labor pains awaiting the birth of what God is doing. It bothers me that we seem to have attempted to redirect Jesus' emphasis from redeeming the Earth to escaping it! Then again, how else could we sell so many copies of Left Behind?

We listen to Jesus when he prays, "thy will be done on Earth as it is in heaven." The Lord's Prayer clearly reveals that Jesus' task is to bring the kingdom of God to Earth; the main sphere of kingdom activity is to be on Earth. Why? Because the Earth needs help to become what God had in mind for it. I cannot help but remember comedian Jon Stewart's 2004 commencement address to the College of William and Mary, his alma mater. He said, "I don't really know how to put this, so I'll be blunt. We broke [the world]. Please don't be mad. I know we're supposed to bequeath to the next generation a world better than the one we were handed. So sorry…But here's the good news. You fix this thing. You're the next greatest generation, people." Stewart was right: the world is broken and this generation has an opportunity to fix it. It has been broken a long time, though; we were not the first generation to fail to clean up this mess. But we all have the opportunity to help fix it now through our partnership with God who has long sought to fix all of creation.

We could also say that we have lost the Garden of Eden and God has been working with us to bring it back. We experienced Genesis 3 and we desire to experience Revelation 21 and 22. This is known as "tikkun olam" (to fix or mend what is broken) by our Jewish brothers and sisters. The rabbis of Jesus' era described "shalom" as a world in which everything works together in the beauty and harmony God intended. They saw the kingdom of God as God's act in turning the chaos of our world back into shalom. Wherever we find illness, disease, hunger, injustice, loneliness, broken relationships, and oppression, we are experiencing chaos. God wants our partnership; God wants to work through us and accomplish a turn in creation toward shalom.

Some rabbis talked about this participation in the kingdom of God as the opportunity to become co-creators with God. They argue that God left some things in chaos on purpose to give us the opportunity to act as co-creators. Regardless of whether or not that theology holds true, that God is working to restore creation to God's perfect shalom and that we are invited to join in the effort is an ancient and biblical idea. N.T. Wright in his book *Simply Christian* calls this effort "God's rescue operation." God is rescuing all of creation by restoring it to its original design. This notion of the kingdom is more fulfilling and exciting to me than just waiting to die so that I can get to a place called heaven.

Decades ago, Ralph Stockman, a famous preacher, observed that there are two kinds of people in the world: those who want to make a better world and those who want to make a better place for themselves in the world as it is. It seems to me that our church often emphasizes sermons and programs that help people survive, even thrive, in the world as it is. There is certainly a place for that. Our faith brings us comfort and guidance for this life and its troubles, but I long for a day when churches will see their role in what their heavenly Father is doing: restoring and re-creating a better world.

We return to the Lord's Prayer one more time. "Our Father" comes before "your kingdom come." The words "Our Father" remind us that our kingdom work comes out of our relationship with the Father and our identity as heirs. "Our" also reminds us that our kingdom efforts should be done communally. It seems possible that any good efforts at restoring beauty and shalom that are attempted apart from community may not actually be restorative because restoration involves community both as the means and the goal of our efforts. Herod used others to build his dream. They were not partners in his efforts. The Father invites us to work on projects together with Him that will fulfill His plan for creation. Herod's projects benefited, for the most part, only Herod, but the Father's projects benefit the co-creators and the ones for whom the project is intended to save.

A critical component of our participation in the advancement of God's kingdom is doing what the Father *does*, doing what the Father *wants done*, and doing it all in the *way* the Father wants it done. Jesus confessed to the disciples, "I can only do what I see the Father doing." Herod was all about his own plans and methods; this serves as an important reminder that church leaders must seek the Father's will before they develop their own plans and strategies. We too often come up with wonderful plans and strategies and then take them to the Father to receive blessing. Yet, there is something else here that runs even more counter to our Western notions of discipleship and kingdom building; Jesus was carrying out the Father's mission, and then the disciples carried out Jesus' mission, which was the Father's mission. It all returns to the Father's will. Normally we (Christians) decide what we believe God tells us our mission is, and we go out to accomplish it; we may even do it in community with others. We carry out our mission as we understand it. We figure it out for ourselves, and then we carry it out by our own authority and strength.

I have too often passed on Frederick Buechner's helpful advice to Christians looking for a place to serve: "Find the place where your deep joy and the world's great need intersect" (*Wishful Thinking*). Many good deeds have been done this way for kingdom advancement. It is part of our Protestant heritage to listen to God's leading and figure out how to follow it, but what I see in Jesus and the disciples is significantly different. They sought to serve the mission Jesus discerned from the Father, and they discovered their place of service within that mission. I trust my spiritual parents to discern the mission given to them in accordance with the heavenly Father's kingdom mission, and then I find my place of service within it through prayer and discernment. We normally administer gifts tests or personality surveys to new-hires in church leadership and then release people to find their own mission, which is usually a task we had in mind for them. We should instead release people to find their mission under the larger mission that the spiritual leaders of the church have discerned from the Father. These ministers to the kingdom mission go out into the world with freedom and responsibility; they are free to serve under the authority of the church fathers' mission discernment, to which they are responsible.

It starts with me as the senior pastor submitting to my father (the bishop) and his understanding of the heavenly Father's mission. With the Spirit's and the community's help, I discern our church's place within the spiritual father's mission. Then the various leaders within our church find their places within the church's vision. Many Protestants will be suspicious of this method, and understandably so. We're not used to being asked to submit to earthly spiritual authority. I understand that, and I have the pirate flag to prove it! Others will worry about the abuse of spiritual authority, which is at times a sad reality in the Christian world. But in my experience, this aligning of the leaders under the father's vision brings clarity, unity, and freedom. It inspires me to make sure that I am clear about our particular mission under the heavenly Father and the bishop's vision, and it intensifies my efforts and longing to support our people in finding and carrying out the piece of the vision that they have been given.

Six years ago, our church got involved in a mission to Burundi in Africa. Burundi is next to Rwanda, and it is recovering from the same kind of civil war and genocide that plagued Rwanda. If you have seen the movie Hotel Rwanda, you have probably seen images of the Motel Burundi. We support a new denomination called the Evangelical Free Baptist Church of Burundi. This denomination came out of the Baptist Church of Burundi following the end of the war in 2005, but they are organized more like Methodists—with a bishop and ten regional supervisors. The church was formed out of a desire to extend the church's reach outside the capital city of Bujumbura and into all seventeen of the country's provinces. It sought to take part in the rebuilding of the country after the devastation wrought by the war. We send a team every year to Burundi to train pastors, educate lay leaders, and monitor and encourage the orphanage we help support My role in this mission is to carry out their bishop's plans for our participation and to support our team leader, Clarence Bray, in the mission. Clarence is a member of our congregation and a member of the small group I take part in. Clarence discovers the bishop's desires and mission for us, and I do all I can to submit to those plans and honor them. I teach many leaders and preach many sermons in their churches around Burundi, but I do this under the vision of the Bishop and of Clarence. Their leadership and understanding of the mission gives me great freedom to use my gifts in my participation. I do not feel restrained in any way in my service to their mission; rather, I find clarity about my distinct role.

I have learned how to discover my spiritual parents in any given situation and devote my attention and efforts to serving the mission God has given them. You may be wondering whether or not I have to hammer other people into a shape that fits into the vision that God has given me under our Bishop. No. I have found that those under me, who see me as their spiritual father, encourage and challenge their siblings to support the mission of the house. My job has mainly been one of support and encouragement. I will come back to that later.

As many leaders will tell you, one of the best ways to learn to be a good leader is to become a good follower. Serving under a spiritual parent's mission is the best way to prepare yourself to become a spiritual parent. I used to think God's call to leaders only came 'out of the blue' in a time of need, but now I wonder if God's call also comes to those who are trained as servants for another person's mission. I see this kind of call in David of the biblical story "David and Goliath"; David serves his brothers and their commanders and is eventually called forward to fight Goliath, the giant. I also see this kind of call in some of the disciples, including Andrew, who were disciples of John the Baptist; they served his mission until Jesus called them. Philip was "sitting under the fig tree," which is an allusion to "studying under a Rabbi," when Jesus first saw him. James and John were serving in their father's fishing business when Jesus called them. In the next chapter, I will share the blessings that have come to me as a result of my service to the mission of my spiritual fathers, rather than as a result of my service to my own mission.

Another reason why we should serve out of our identity as an heir in the family business is that destructive results often come in our lives when we act as orphans. The negative results are even more magnified when an entire church (or denomination!) acts with orphaned hearts. Let us revisit a few of the behaviors we notice in orphan-hearted people and explore a few new ones that relate specifically to the church:

Drivenness: Often what masquerades as passion in church leaders is really just drivenness fueled by lack of identity and a sense of low self-worth. One of the downsides of receiving the mandate known as the Great Commission is that we act as if our place in God's family is dependent upon recruiting others into the family. I earnestly desire for all persons to know the joy and peace that comes from being a child of God, and that desire fuels my evangelistic fervor. I reach out to others out of a sense of belonging and worth in the hope that they can experience that same wonderful home that I experience. I do not reach out to others because I feel that my place is dependent upon their response. I remember Trevor Hudson telling me that if we reach out to others without the sense of our own identity and acceptance, our witness will be both ineffective and unhealthy. To use Martin Buber's great metaphor, operating outside of our own acceptance will lead us to see and treat others as "its" not "thous." Our work, like Herod before us, will be largely impersonal. Drivenness is also powered by guilt, and guilt is not helpful motivation. When used as a motivation, it does not respect the freedom of another person to respond. Guilt is used as a form of manipulation and control. How often have we Christians heard well-meaning messages decrying our inability to keep up with the growth of the population or lamenting the loss of today's youth in Christianity?

While true on an intellectual level, these laments do not ultimately respect the heart and its freedom to choose. Freely chosen evangelism will trump guilt-driven evangelism every time.

Drivenness might also lead us to overplay our role in the process. We act as if we are the ones bringing God's kingdom to fruition. True, we have a role to play, but God is driving this bus. We get an opportunity to partner with God and others along the journey. We often confuse our actions with God's actions. God initiates; we respond. My drivenness may actually have a negative effect on the person whom I claim to value in evangelism. I make people important only in their response and do not value people as they currently exist.

Guilt: As I previously mentioned, I believe guilt is often linked to our driven behavior. We're trying to reach people with the good news, which includes the news that they are absolved from guilt. It seems hypocritical that guilt is often a seemingly important factor in spreading the message of absolution and freedom.

Fear: Much of our church's behavior seems to flow from the feeling of fear that if we do not perform at a certain level, our organization may cease to exist. This insecurity belies our lack of assurance about our place in the Father's house. I have a hunch that our churches act more often out of fear than love—fear about lack of resources, fear about our future survival, and fear about our current relevance or irrelevance. I know that I am personally never my best self when I'm acting out of fear; I cannot imagine that my church is either. Fear tends to place programs over relationships and survival over mission. Walk around the church; how many conversations are about risk and taking chances? How many of the conversations are about surviving and protecting our assets? As a leader, I can be sucked into fear pretty quickly; I watch numbers instead of individuals and relationships and worry about where we may be in a few years down the road, but I miss the opportunity to love and live boldly in the present. How often have I sat in a church meeting regarding finances and assumed that God's resources were a fixed pie or a zero-sum game? "You can add staff or increase missions giving, but you cannot do both." Just once, I would like to say, "I will choose both and see if God honors that choice," or, "Yes. We might go bankrupt, but there are worse ways to do that than giving money away." But I haven't. I'm afraid to.

Competition: Heirs to the riches of the universe can be among the most competitive people in existence. Some competition is healthy; it can bring out the best in us. It can rally the troops. However, we may need to redefine what we mean by "competition." Our competition is not the other churches or the "pagan" culture that leads people away from God. Jesus saw this as a battle of kingdoms. We compete to help free people who are oppressed by the evil kingdom through sickness, poverty, broken relationships, and injustice. We compete in the cause of the freedom and the peace God intends, not because we fear we will lose our place in the house but because we are a part of the kingdom competition—a victory for any church or charity is a victory for us all!

Control and Manipulation: When church leaders behave in a controlling manner, they give a pretty clear signal that they do not have the security of being an heir in the house. Something unique about our church's leadership is that we tend not to make long-term strategic plans. We try to be open to what God is doing at this moment in time. As Henry Blackaby used to say, "We look for what the Father is doing and try to join in" (*Experiencing God*). Most of the really wonderful things that have happened in our church were not a result of our plans but a result of our receptiveness to what God was doing in that instance. One of the ways I describe it is as follows: it is not my job as a son to push the doors open but to have the courage to walk through the doors that the Father has opened for me. We are learning to move into the future that God has provided instead of the one we create. This is not to advocate irresponsibility; we stress that preparation is a virtue. We are also learning to respect the freedom of others to respond or not to respond to our leadership. While we may talk about submission, it is clearly an invitation and not an injunction.

So how can we try to combat our orphan tendencies and act out of our identity as the Beloved in the church? Here again, I find the parable of the loving father in Luke 15 of great assistance. How does the father (who we could argue really acts as a beloved son) exercise his leadership?

The father *creates an environment that allows both of his sons to grow*. Both sons are given freedom and unconditional love. Both appear to make poor choices. The younger son chooses to leave home and deny his identity; the older chooses not to honor the identity of his younger brother when he returns home. Both, however, continue to receive the father's love unconditionally.

The father *allows both sons to fail.* One of the ways that the kingdom advances is through the bold acts of people—calls to action they have received from God. This unhindered action can only come about when the fear of failure has been removed from the equation. We give our leaders at the church long leashes that are tethered to the father's mission.

The father *runs to the sons but does not run after them.* Again, the father respects the freedom of the sons to choose how they will respond to him. At the same time, he does not allow their responses to determine his own worth or value as a parent. He does not seem to be worried about the fact that the village would appear scandalized by the younger son's departure and that his employees might question his authority when the older son refuses his invitation to join the party for the return of the younger son. We never want to base our value on the way others respond to us, but we want to be ready to receive them with open arms. If people run away from our church, we can only allow that, but we want to be the first person to reach out when they make their way back. We keep the lights on for them—we look out for them always.

The father *celebrates their identity* as heirs. We believe it is more helpful to address people as sons rather than sinners and as daughters rather than demons. Rabbi Akiva once quipped, "The great sin of the rabbis is to teach people to believe in God without teaching them that God believes in them." Just as it has been critical to picture God as Father before picturing God as King in our quest to grasp our identity, it is also critical to see people as children before we see them as sinners. We must treat them in a way that reinforces their identity in Christ.

The father *allows consequences*. The father does not punish the sons for wrong choices, but he does allow the younger son to experience the consequences of his choices. His inheritance is spent, but his place in the family is secure. Sometimes I think that we in America are more into punishment than we are into consequences. The guilty party must be identified and punished when something goes wrong. We seem to be quick to fire church workers and public officials for mistakes instead of allowing them to make amends for the mistake and grow as a person.

We seem almost to take pride in how swiftly the offender was terminated from their leadership position in the church or in the government. To me, this does not do anything to honor personal identity and the image of God within each person. Yes, there are consequences for mistakes, but it too often seems as though we remove any possibility of redemption and restitution upon recognizing the mistake.

The father *avoids shaming his sons*. The father does not question the intrinsic value and worth of his sons even when they choose poorly. Shame makes us feel unworthy of being in community with others—unworthy of being in the family. We try to lead our church in a way that protects the value and worth of people, but we are not always successful. Shaming is to deny a person's identity as an heir. It leads to orphan behavior and it is an unworthy and unhelpful motivational tool.

The father *leaves an inheritance for his sons*. One of the things good leadership will do is leave a healthy legacy and an inheritance for the next generation. The legacy that I want to leave the future leaders of this church is one of belief in the importance of loving relationships. People really can act and live productively in a loving manner! I also want to encourage those who come after me to trust God and others; I want to leave a legacy of kept promises. A spiritual father keeps the promises he makes to the children.

Herod left his sons a wealthy kingdom in turmoil. He changed his will at least six times and killed the heirs who were most capable of succeeding him. They were overwhelmed and underprepared for what they had to face. They were left as orphaned as Herod was, if not more. Like their father before them, they turned to Rome for help. Unlike their father, however, their kingdoms did not prosper. They did not received the kind of inheritance in love, security, and guidance necessary to rule in his place.

The inheritance I hope to leave to my church will be little compared to the inheritance all of us have already received at AHUMC. I will share the story of that inheritance in the next chapter. We did not do it “the old fashioned way”; we did not earn it. We received it.

CHAPTER SEVEN

Receiving an Inheritance

~

There is a story about a rabbi and his somewhat arrogant disciple. One day the Rabbi began to pour tea into the disciple's cup until it overflowed and fell to the ground. When the disciple protested, the rabbi said, "Your cup is too full to receive anything from me." I look at my days of orphan leadership in this way. I was full of my plans, my desires, and my needs for attention. I was the arrogant disciple whose cup was too full to receive God's gifts. The same was true for our church. I also picture a closed fist when I reflect on my orphaness; when I was busy taking hold of what I could grasp out of my efforts and clutching tightly to what I had already gained for fear of losing it, I was unable to receive from God. Again, the same was true for our church; as long as we were concerned with holding onto what we had in financial resources, human resources, programs, and facilities, we were missing the opportunity to receive the growth and life God wanted to give.

In the most humble manner I can, I want to tell you about some of what we have received as a church and what I have received as a pastor/leader since we moved from the Herodian style grasping of an orphan to the receiving style of a beloved son or daughter. I say "humble" because none of this is due to our seemingly wise strategies. This inheritance may not seem anywhere near as significant to you as it does to us, but I want to share it with you nonetheless.

THE QUARRY

I cannot talk about life and ministry at AHUMC without discussing The Quarry. God moved here in ways that far exceeded anything I could have planned. In 2008, Scott and I began to talk about the possibility of training pastoral leaders in our local context. We know that many people who feel called to pastoral ministry cannot afford to leave home and go to seminary. We are also often concerned about the ability of seminaries to equip graduates with on the ground, concrete training necessary to thrive in church leadership. The notion that a person who feels called to be in church leadership would have to leave their community to study in a place hundreds of miles away and then return to pastor a different community seems to be at odds with what we were learning about leadership and community. Scott and I talked about how we would love to have the opportunity to gather the people who we knew felt called into ministry and provide them with ministry training.

Then, at the 2009 meeting of our Methodist annual conference, our hope turned into a calling of our own. Bishop James Dorf stressed the need for recruiting younger leaders into ministry and the need to create new places for ministry. We knew that we were being called not only to train leaders but also to allow them the freedom to form new faith communities, or "lighthouses" as we started calling them. The churches planted by leaders or brought under the direction of those leaders in our training group would become a network of house churches formed out of and supported by AHUMC. We met with our bishop, our spiritual father, and received his approval to start administering this training in 2010.

We called it "The Quarry" for two reasons: first, our church had relocated to a former rock quarry, and second, this name reminds us of one of our favorite verses in Isaiah chapter 51: "Look to the rock from which you were cut and to the quarry from which you were hewn: look to Abraham, your father, and to Sarah, who gave you birth" (NIV). Our original plan for The Quarry was to invite people who had indicated to us that they felt a call to the pastoral ministry. We figured that twelve would be a nice biblical number to begin with, but that number quickly turned into sixteen and then the sixteen invited others. We also intended that the process would last two and a half years and focus on character, theory, and skills; as our friend and father in leadership, retired Lieut. Gen. Tom Jaco, called it "be, know, do"—a saying derived from his Army experience. But here again, God had slightly different plans. Our group expanded to a total of thirty-five in regular attendance. At the end of the first two and a half year cycle, more than fifty people participated with some degree of regularity. We're also surprised that out of the group of fifty, only seven wanted to enter candidacy for pastoral ministry in the United Methodist Church. A large number wanted instead to remain in the training and in community of support in order to continue discerning what God was calling them to be in the world.

Scott began to say that The Quarry gave people confidence for their calling. It felt as if we hung a single target to the wall but hit a different target right in the bull's-eye! We were also surprised that people did not desire to graduate from The Quarry. As we planned our second cycle start date for September 2012, we realized that our alumni wanted to continue learning in this community. I was as surprised at how much The Quarry meant to me personally as I was at what it meant to the group. I felt affirmed and challenged and this group helped me to live out of a place of acceptance and rest. My identity as the beloved was secure in the acceptance I felt in that community, and out of that security, I could risk more. We could cover topics at a much deeper level, and I could freely offer what might be considered a strange or a minority opinion without fear. I was learning to apply my insight into the Jewish roots of our faith, information I learned in seminary, in a way that was Spirit-led. That insight led me to places that were not normally considered mainline or evangelical. They also led me to freedom (more on that in chapters eight and nine).

Perhaps the biggest surprise God had in store for us in the creation of The Quarry was the interest it drew from outside our church community. None of our talks went viral on YouTube, and we didn't make any big newspaper headlines. People were not clamoring for us to become a teaching church and hold a conference for thousands of people to attend. But we drew interest from a seminary. My alma mater, Duke Divinity School, heard about The Quarry. Their online publication

"Faith and Leadership" already wrote a story on Riverside in 2010 called "Coffeehouse Church," but this time they sent a team of researchers to interview our Quarry participants and leaders and produce a study to help us reflect and to guide us on our journey ahead. Then, in 2013, they published an article about us for their online publication. Their support and feedback helped us as we wrestled with The Quarry's future direction and gave us the confidence that we were onto something special.

My shame voice spoke out of my orphan heart and told me that The Quarry was just a glorified adult Bible study—and not a very good one at that! But soon, other pastors began asking about the Quarry. We are currently in the preliminary discussion about what it would look like to expand The Quarry to three other locations. The Quarry keeps growing and gaining recognition, and my shame voice is told over and over again to "Sit down, and hush!"

When I'm asked to describe the Quarry I give this explanation: it is a kingdom leadership training process that takes place in community and is grounded in our identity as children of God; it is informed by the Jewish roots of Jesus, and it is committed to the Father's mission of partnering with the Spirit in the task of advancing the kingdom of God on Earth. I know that is a mouthful, but it is a pretty good definition of the way I have come to see church—a way that is drastically different from the way I defined it years ago.

RIVERSIDE COMMUNITY CHURCH

One of the most exciting things God has given to us is our Riverside campus. Riverside was conceived in 2003 when we had finally given up trying to tell God what we wanted our future to be. Before this, in 2002, we formed a strategic planning team; we met together regularly and read the latest books by church consultants and church growth experts. However, we found that we could not identify and agree on a future direction for our church. We disbanded as the strategic *planning* team and came back together later as a strategic *listening* team. We decided to put our books away and seek God in prayer instead. We wanted to hear what God wanted us to do. Not long after, three of our members, all within 48-hours of each other, received the same leading from God. One was in San Antonio at the time, one was in Chicago at leadership conference, and one was in Missouri on a family farm. The message we received was this: we were not to expand on our current campus; we were to start a new campus. Our church was founded in 1910 and it was relocated in 1994 to the place it now stands. One of our members termed this a "chapter 3" for our church. We moved off the campus again, but we maintained the current site.

Having heard a message we believed was from God, I kicked back into my planning mode. I wanted to pick a geographic location that made demographical sense for the campus. I picked our intern, Michael, to be the pastor of this new campus. With my fist tight and my cup full, I started to move forward. Scott came into my office one day to announce that God told him he was supposed to lead this new campus. "No," I told him. "Michael will lead it." But God soon began to make it clear that God, not me, would choose a leader. Scott was the leader. Michael led the New Heights community after Scott left to go to the new campus. God also chose the place—a place no demographic study indicated to us—and as for the method we would use to start this new church, God seemed to say, "Don't even go there." Riverside was God's baby from the beginning in every way imaginable.

How would the church start? God had some ideas there as well. Instead of working toward opening a worship service at a local school or theater, God moved Scott and the leaders to start at a coffee shop called the Loft. Scott, upon returning from a trip to Israel, was pondering the concept of shephelah. In ancient Israel, Shephelah was the middle ground between the pagans on the coastal plain and the Jews who live in the hills. This meeting area was a place where people of different faiths would come together. It was the task of the Jews to live and act in a way that would spark interest in those outside their faith. Scott knew our church needed to create a shephelah—a place that needed not to simply serve as a retreat in the hills for the already convinced. He pondered that concept at a local Starbucks near our church one day where he liked to hang out and meet people. He saw a poster on the wall that said, "Create community." Then and there, God gave birth to our Riverside campus.

One day Scott was driving up a highway about twenty miles north of our campus when he noticed an old house and a barn for lease. The owner of the property was disappointed to learn that Scott was from a church and that he did not really have the authority to make any agreements about leasing retail property, but he showed Scott around anyways. As they came to the back porch of the house, Scott noticed a woman painting from a ladder. The owner joked, "You're from a church; that woman needs prayer." Sometime later, Linda, one of our other leaders who eventually became a pastor at the Riverside campus, went to look at that property also. She pulled up in a nice vehicle, better than the one Scott had arrived in, and again the owner hoped to make a sale. He was again disheartened to learn that this woman came from our church and that she also had no authority to enter into a leasing agreement. However, this woman of faith was carrying $1300 in her purse. She felt a call from God to raise money for a single mother in our community for whom she raised $2600. But the woman had insisted on only taking half of the money from Linda.

When Linda and the property owner got to the back porch after touring the property, they saw the same woman—Pam—painting. "You're from a church," the owner joked to Linda. "See that woman? She needs prayer." "Well, do you?" Linda asked Pam. Pam indicated that she was in need of prayer. Linda prayed and talked with her; as it turned out, the woman was painting because she had lost her job. She was a single mom who was in need of money to pay her bills, which came to the amount of…$1300! With great joy, Linda announced that their meeting was an act of God. Linda gave the money to Pam who was gushing with thanks and was intrigued by these church people who so willingly responded to God. Pam later joined our church and became one of the early leaders at Riverside. Today, she runs our Hope Center and Thrift Shop for Riverside; she helps people in need get back on their feet in the same way God helped her through Linda.

It was clear to us from this miraculous situation with Pam that this place was meant to be the long-term home of our new faith community. It was not where we would have placed it or where our denominational officers and demographic experts would have led us; but it was God's pick—a miraculous and perfect pick.

ASBURY

In 2011, God again had plans to expand our campus in a way we would not have planned. For a few years, I wrestled with the uncomfortable realization that both of our campuses were outside the city center. Our main campus is suburban in the fairly affluent part of San Antonio; Riverside might be considered ex-urban—surrounded by great affluence and pockets of areas dominated by the working poor. One day, the district superintendent asked if AHUMC would be interested in taking over Asbury church, where one of our former interns served as a part-time pastor. It was a few miles closer in town and its membership had dwindled to about twelve worshipers, most of whom were octogenarians and were not physically able to reach the changing neighborhood around them. We began to work with Asbury by sending youth choirs to sing and volunteer crews to paint and refurbish the aging facilities.

But when we grew more aggressive about outreach and attempted to facilitate a Vacation Bible School with the community around Asbury, including children whom we would bus in from a community center that helped the underserved, the church board told the pastor to cut us off. Our plans to be a partner congregation with Asbury had failed, but now the denomination was trying to give it to us over the objections of the church board. In May of 2011, the superintendent asked us to take the church over from top to bottom; I was willing to accept, but I told him that I would talk with the administrative board about it. I began to talk to Scott about all the things we could do on this new campus. He reminded me that we might want to pray about it first! We both laughed because that's usually what I have to tell him. We had indeed gotten ahead of ourselves. The church, fearing the AHUMC takeover, negotiated with the superintendent for another year on its own.

We spent that year getting to know the part-time pastor, Robert Ortiz, and looking for ways to encourage him. Janet, one of our leaders from The Quarry began to assist him. She became like a second pastor to Asbury, and we were eventually able to merge with Asbury in July 2012. They now have a Sunday morning worship that is more than fifty percent Hispanic, a recovery service on Saturday night, and a smaller service on Sunday night. Susan, a former member of AHUMC and ordained pastor, volunteered to assist Robert as well. Susan and Robert now work to build the relationship between the community and the church. Stories of miraculous, life-changing occurrences are beginning to flow back to our main campus from Asbury, and we are all greatly encouraged by what is happening there. This mutually enriching connection between our campuses and Ashbury would not have been possible if we tried to do it our own way. We did not find it by looking for it; we simply walked into the opportunity unknowingly, and God gave us everything we needed to build that relationship.

OUR ECONOMIC STIMULUS PACKAGE

I would love to tell you that as we began to live into our identity as heirs, we received an overabundance of financial resources with which to carry on the kingdom work and family business of our Father. I would love to tell you that my greatest challenge is trying to decide what to do with the financial windfall we have received, but that isn't how it happened for us. However, even without the benefit of a hard-driving, super organized financial campaign, God has provided enough resources for to us to do our job as His church. For example, the year we took on the Asbury campus, we invested $150,000 in it; want to guess the exact amount of surplus funds we ended the year with? $150,000, of course! We even managed to save enough money to cover about three months' worth of operating expenses at Asbury. I can't say that I no longer worry about funds, but I worry less than I used to. With God as our economic stimulus package, who needs a Herod?

Secondly, I can tell you that while God has given us enough funds to do the work, God has also given us amazing human resources. God sent to our community an expert in ancient languages; I had wanted to take Hebrew ever since returning from my 2007 trip to Israel, and

Jonah was willing and able to teach a few of us Hebrew for one year. We were also blessed with Gayle, a PhD candidate in early Christian origins. Gayle teaches on Jewish history and culture and teaches us how we, as Christians, can celebrate the Jewish festivals. God also gave us Susan, who volunteered her pastoral skills and experience at Asbury. Through The Quarry, we met Chris who has been sober for fourteen years and has led us into ministry with people who suffer from addiction. He also leads our Pioneer recovery group and worship service at Asbury. Chris enlightens us with his experience in AA at our weekly pastors' text discussions. All of these blessings in human form remind me that the greatest inheritance I enjoy is the ability to celebrate the growth of my children in the faith. The God-given human resources of our church could fill another book, and it would likely be a more entertaining read, but I will leave it at that for now.

FAITHWALKING

Another transformative experience God surprised us with is called Faithwalking. It started in 2007 in Houston, Texas under the leadership of Jim Herrington. We first heard about it from Jim Turley of the Texas Methodist Foundation. Turley enthusiastically described it as a discipleship process that was beginning to make a significant impact on its participants. We, like all churches, wrestle with the concept of discipleship. We seem to know more what it is not than what it is. We are sure it is not only a series of classes based on insight and information but that it must also involve a more Jesus-like combination of relationships, experience, and mentoring. Faithwalking seemed to offer all of that.

We met Jim Herrington for lunch in Katy Texas in the spring of 2012, and his words both challenged and encouraged us. We could sense that Faithwalking was not your basic spiritual renewal retreat. As I later explained to our church, "We are not going to sit around and sing Kum Ba Yah." Having experienced Faithwalking 101 and 201, I would describe it as a discipleship process that results in inner transformation for the purpose of participating in community transformation (i.e. the kingdom of God—the family business). Here is Faithwalking's official description:

> Faithwalking is creating a community of disciples of Jesus who are personally being transformed and becoming catalysts mobilizing Christians to become the

> functioning body of Christ in their neighborhoods, workplaces, and the third places to serve the poor, the marginalized, and those in need, to work for the common good, and to restore individuals, social systems, communities, and nations to God's design (Faithwalking.us).

Herrington and his team led a weekend 101 retreat at our church in September 2012, though that was not the normal Faithwalking procedure. Sixty people from our three campuses gathered for the retreat in our church gym. It was a profound experience for all of us.

Thirty-seven people of the sixty who attended 101 signed up for 201, which is a six-month process involving class sessions, coaching groups, and experiential homework. More than twenty of the 201 participants were staff members at AHUMC. We used to joke, "Faithwalking Sucks!" It did suck. It was extremely difficult, but the Holy Spirit was working in profound ways. It was one of the most profound experiences of my life. I still have a long way to go, but God has used the Faithwalking process to lead me to a greater boldness, vulnerability, and persistence. I doubt I would have finished this book were it not for Faithwalking's challenge to my sense of shame and my practice of procrastination. Once again, the best things God planned for us were not a result of our grasping or strategizing. We are now working with Jim Herrington to expand the Faithwalking opportunities for our community and our city.

ALL MY CHILDREN

My twenty-one-year-old son preached recently for one of our services. Though his calling is not higher than that of my other two sons, I was extremely proud of his willingness to begin living out his calling to pastoral ministry. We are called to serve God in a variety of places, and I am grateful for the places to which all of my children, biological and spiritual, are called. Watching my biological son preach was not the first time in which I experienced the great sense of gratification that overflowed in me that day.

One of the best gifts that has come to me through living as a beloved son to our Father is the gift of my many spiritual sons and daughters here in the AHUMC family. These spiritual children include the more than thirty participants in The Quarry and a group of eighteen people who preach on occasion at one of our AHUMC family's eleven weekend worship services. I meet with this group of eighteen preachers every Tuesday to discuss the Scripture text for the coming week, and I am continually amazed and blessed by their passion for and insight into the text.

When I am able to witness any of my spiritual children preach, I feel as proud of them as if I were their biological father. This group has also given me life in a profound and unexpected way: through the power of prayer. Before my last trip to Africa, they each prayed over me and assured me that nothing would skip a beat at AHUMC or its various campuses while I was out of town. They prayed over me when I was in need of assurance and peace and shared that they were each there to support me as loving and loyal sons and daughters.

When I first arrived at AHUMC in 1995, I had no idea that my time with pastoral leaders would be the most significant blessing and opportunity of my ministry. Now, as I watch them lead and give birth to new expressions of ministry, I feel the joy that I imagine a grandparent must feel watching their children and grandchildren thrive. In the summer of 2013, my youngest biological son, Reed, spent five weeks interning in Columbia, South Carolina with one of my former interns.

My biological son interned with my intern—my spiritual son! When he preached in our sanctuary upon returning from his internship, he did so without shoes in homage to Pastor Scott. Reed acknowledged that Scott was his role model. Was I offended? No! I was so very proud of my biological son. Reed looks up to and supports the efforts of my spiritual sons. Does it get any better than that? My life feels so much larger than I ever imagined it could be—not Herodian large, complete with buildings, power, wealth, and acclaim, but Kingdom-with-a-capital-K large, overflowing with love and a living legacy.

CHAPTER EIGHT

From Herod to Heir: A Constant Transformation

~

This practice of living more as heirs than as orphans has begun to take hold in our leadership circles. Here is what some of the leaders in The Quarry say about the difference acting as an heir has made in their lives:

"It has made me a better person."—Joni

"God's love has been a revelation!"—Donna

"I can get to a place where I don't worry."—Fred

"Sonship is a tool to freedom."—Colin

"Artists are insecure and can't play well with others. Sonship has totally transformed the way I lead worship."—Adam, worship leader

"I will risk more because I have a home." —Scott

"I have let God run my business, but I still have fear and need to stay in community."—Chris

Chris's comment reveals the truth about all of us as we continue to struggle in this transformation from Herod to heir. We do not have this all figured out. We are not completely free, but we are moving in that direction.

Darrell, one of our Quarry members, articulated his experience living as an heir, which he calls "sonship." His words accurately reflect the experience of many in The Quarry:

> I wish I could say that I have stopped striving altogether, but I have not. Even still, there are hundreds of times each day when I have an opportunity to behave as a striving orphan or as a loved and safe son of the Most High. It is a good day when I ultimately choose my sonship at a majority of those intersections. In spite of this reality, I can testify to new and increasing levels of freedom, peace, rest, and clarity of calling.
>
> When I catch myself striving or responding with guilt, fear, or anxiety, I now have the tools and experience to step back and try to understand where I stepped off the

path of the truth and started walking in a lie. Without fail, that path leads me back to a choice I made to doubt my safety, my worthiness, my purpose, or my access to unconditional love. In every instance, the Spirit encourages me to see that I am "orphaning-out" because I believe one area of my fulfillment—my unconditional love from the Lord, my safety in the Lord, my value to the Lord, or my purpose and calling in the Lord—is threatened.

Every time I choose sonship, I discover a little more of the overwhelming provision and protection of God. As my familiarity with the divine identity increases, my understanding of my personal identity and my relationship to God and God's people grows deeper. How much blood, how much sweat, and how many tears have I shed in attempt to gain the approval of the created when I was born with the approval of the creator?

Darrell's description almost sounds too good to be true. But it is true. That does not mean it will be universally accepted, though. Jesus lived as an heir in complete freedom, and he was crucified! When the future we construct is confronted with a future we cannot control, we are tempted to reject the future we are confronted with—no matter how good it turns out to be. My sense is that as we live more freely as heirs, we will face far less outside persecution. We, as Christians living in America, will not likely face death. At worst, people will be confused by our freedom and joy, and at best, they will be attracted to our freedom and joy. The real threat to our freedom comes from within. The pull toward orphan behavior will continue to be strong. I will be continually tempted to get back on the performance treadmill. The reality of unconditional acceptance and a secure home with the Father will seem too good to be true. Herod will look more appealing than Jesus. I find Darrell's words helpful here again as he compares our struggle to live as heirs rather than orphans to the situation Eddie Murphy's character faces in the movie *Trading Places*:

My attempt to grasp my sonship reminds me a lot of Eddie Murphy's character in the movie *Trading Places*. The Duke Brothers and their butler bring the street hustler (Murphy) into their lavish mansion, clean him up, dress him in the finest suits, and try to convince him that they are giving him all of these riches and a job working for them. They plead with Murphy to accept his new status in the middle of an opulent formal living room, which now belongs to Murphy. He smiles and nods his head as though he agrees with their outlandish proposal but steals various decorations and trinkets from the room. He doesn't believe it. He thinks that any minute, the joke will be up, and he will be back out on the street fighting for his life again. So he keeps working. He is still on the job. Though he is surrounded by everything he needs and is being offered the opportunity to enter into partnership with those who could fully provide for and protect him, he continues to steal.

Coming to grips with my identity as a son who does not have to scrape, scratch, and strive to survive was neither instantaneous nor is it complete. I've had to grow in my trust of the Lord to provide the things I believed I had to obtain for myself. What that looks like in my life is a continual experiment. I'd like to say it's like one of those "faith falls" where you turn your back to a group of people, close your eyes, and fall backwards trusting than they catch you. But it has been nothing like that. Don't get me wrong, I believe completely that if I were to turn my back, close my eyes, and fall into sonship, the Lord would catch me; in fact, I'm assured of that truth by Scripture. The problem is not that I am unsure whether or not the Lord will catch me; the problem is that I don't always fall right. Sometimes I bend my knees and try not to fall. Other times, I throw my hands up, twist around, and try to catch myself. Worst of all, I sometimes refuse to fall at all.

Here's the good news: no matter how I fall, the Lord stays with me. Each time I screw up the fall by not trusting in God's love, God's protection, God's delight in me, and God's calling on my life, I'm still okay. God is still on His throne. The Lord picks me up, dusts me off, smiles at me, and says, "You're okay. Let's try again." As one of my mentors taught me, human beings are the only creatures on Earth who can be convinced to walk by love. So it has been with the path of my sonship. The Lord loves me, step by wobbly step.

Eddie Murphy's character eventually settles into his new status and begins to believe, and so did I. Though it did not happen instantly, the Lord is patient and faithful. Unlike Murphy's character, whose new identity in *Trading Places* was a spontaneous result of a temporary bet, our identity as heirs to the kingdom of God always has been and always will be. Living into that truth is a lifelong journey.

The beautiful things are not just the wonderful things that have happened to us personally; beautiful things have also happened to our community as we have moved away from the ways of an orphan. Here again is Darrell's response to a question I posed: What have you seen our community stumble into since we stopped following the ways of Herod?

> "Stumbled into" is the perfect image of how this journey has progressed. We are infants learning to walk in the loving encouragement of the Father. Even though we are young and sometimes unsure on our feet, overwhelming blessings have been dropped into our lap. I group them in the following categories:
>
> *1. A movement away from fiefdoms or many kingdoms and into a tapestry*: Our community could once be described as an assortment of ministry gangs who all sought to take care of their own, provide for themselves, and ensure their continuation. Sure, all of the ministry or program gangs shared the same physical

church and even occasionally "worked together," but they did so very rarely in humility or at their own expense. For your ministry to survive, and thereby your justification for employment, involvement, and existence, you had to fight for budget money, facilities, and attention. If another program or ministry gang received any of those things, there was less for your gang because there's only so much to go around. The result of this lie was a disjointed, disconnected, un-empowered, and competitive priesthood of all believers that was constantly trying to win in the name of Jesus.

The truth is this: we can't possibly fathom God's economy. Scripture tell us the Lord's storehouses are filled with blessings God longs to give His daughters and sons. We have learned to phrase it this way: “One light does not have to dim for another to shine.” The truth is, when one of us shines, everyone wins. Your success is my success, and your failure is my failure. More importantly, regardless of success or failure, we are all still okay. We all receive the unconditional love of the Lord. We are all eternally safe in our Father's kingdom. Each of us is God's favorite. Each of us is called to partner in and for the kingdom of God.

Our community has grown smaller and tighter. With our five different worshiping communities acting in unison, there should be an even greater possibility of division and competition. But those worshiping communities we have "stumbled into" aren't there because we fought to achieve them; they are there because we stopped acting like orphans by fighting to protect our own kingdom.

We began believing that God was big enough and good enough to provide all of us with what we need. We began living into the truth that God loves us so much that we don't have to worry about our own lives and can give ourselves away to others. In doing so, our tapestry is woven. It's not perfect, and is not complete, but if you stand back and look at it, you can behold its communal beauty.

2. *A clearer awareness of the presence and movement of the Lord*: This one is logical and easy to understand. When we began to live as daughters and sons, we were abandoning the orphan ways and tuning out the orphan voice—the result of which is that we have space to hear and time to listen for the Lord. The work of an orphan is exhausting and never ending. Even when the sun goes down and the orphan tries to rest, the nagging sense is still there to remind you of what you failed to do and what you're going to have to do tomorrow.

The work of a daughter or son is simple (please note that I did not say *easy*). It is simple because your job is to do what you see the Father doing. You don't have to come up with it on your own; you just have to watch it and imitate it. Watching and actively engaging with the Father, being conscious to his presence and following his movements, is now our priority.

3. The freedom to fail: Dallas Willard wrote about one of the lies facing Christians, "God loves me, but he doesn't like me very much when I sin." I would argue that Christians, especially American Christians, also struggle with the lie that, "God loves me but he doesn't like me very much when I *fail*." Here is the truth of the sonship into which we are growing: God loves us! Nothing changes that, nothing decreases it, and nothing will ever make it stop, even for a second. Feel free to fail. Go for it. Leave a son- or daughter-shaped hole in the wall you crash through. The Scripture assures us that not even a collection of our worst failures will knock God off His throne for one second. If we believe that for ourselves, we learn to believe it for our brothers and sisters also. Therefore, your failure does not threaten me; it is an opportunity for me to join you and love you. That's it.

4. Growing toward rest: Another logical conclusion: When you stop striving and abandon the work ethic of a servant to embrace the status of an heir, there is not only time to rest but an embrace that allows it. The Scripture calls it "shalom." Let me be completely honest though: this is a tough one for me and, I think, for most Americans. We do not learn to come by rest naturally in this culture. True rest, shalom, requires us to *be still* and know that He is God. Even if we know that He is God, true rest still requires that we *be still*! Being still is not something that you can just start doing. It takes practice. Our community is learning to engage and wrestle with the spiritual disciplines that heighten our awareness, increase our dependence, and lead to being still.

5. Unexpected blessing: To be clear, our unexpected blessings have nothing to do with those things that we pray for and receive. This is about things we never thought to ask for—things we didn't even know existed. The most common unexpected blessing we receive has been in the form of people. The Lord has brought to us some amazing, loving, and powerful people. The Lord has also brought us hurting, needy, and tired people. Here's the thing: Every person the Lord has dropped into our lap is all of those things.

We are continually amazed at the way in which the Lord blesses us with people and uses us to bless people. Please do not misread this as "our numbers have grown" or we are "winning the attendance battle." That is not what this is about; this is about one amazing person at a time who may or may not stay in our community for the long haul. The blessing is not in whether or not they join the church; the blessing is that even when we are not looking for them, the Lord brings them to us and brings us to them.

Even with all of the blessings that Darrell mentioned—all the blessings we have "stumbled into"—the ways of Herod still call out to me, and I'm always tempted to follow. I am tempted to measure things in terms of "how much" and "how many." When these measurements begin to decline, I begin to experience anxiety. When I receive an email regarding a poor month in terms of financial revenue for our church, I calculate how many months we can continue at the pace we currently take and still have an organization that can function effectively. I think about a number of ways I could help secure our future. My orphan tendencies are activated when attendance at functions declines. I get anxious about The Quarry when we have less than thirty in attendance on Thursday night—even though that is almost twice the number of disciples of Jesus had. I run myself in circles of "what-if's" and feel as though I need to breathe into a paper bag! But then I calm down, breathe deeply, and recall that this is the Father's house. I do not need to secure it. I am not saying that the house will make magical progress if we just sit back and ignore work, but I can be more concerned with the Father's mission in the present if I'm not busy trying to plan out the future.

Darrell's quote, "One light does not have to dim for another to shine," reminds me of one of the most beautiful things about living as an heir: the raising and releasing of people into leadership and mission. The "children" in our AHUMC family are going places I could never go and doing things I could never do. As Pastor Scott says, our desire is that "our ceiling be their floor."

As an orphan, I led in a way that discouraged people from exceeding me in their leadership. I became the bottleneck in the mission of my previous congregations. Just as Herod suppressed his most capable successors, I suppressed mine—in a far less violent way, of course. I suppose I saw their success as a threat to my place in the Father's house—like the older brother in the parable of prodigal son. Living as an heir has changed my view of my role as a pastor and leader. I used to think I had to create the future, anticipate, and solve current and future issues for the organization. Now I concentrate on training and freeing leaders to face and solve the issues they will face in their own areas of ministry. I truly believe that the church as we know it will be radically different in the future, but I do not have to figure that out on my own. I am responsible for raising and releasing sons and daughters who are capable of facing the future challenges and finding appropriate ways to be and live in the midst of those challenges. My "long-range planning" takes place every Thursday night as I lead and support future leaders who will carry on the Father's mission.

I do not want you to think that we leaders just sit around eating bonbons and waiting to be called home. No. Quite the opposite. Because we have experienced the security of home here on Earth, we work to help extend that home and its values across our community and world. We have the freedom in our sense of home to go out and take risks on behalf of the kingdom. We like to describe our work as moving "from rest" and not "for rest"—"from home" and not “to find home.” We can freely share resources because we know that they are the family's resources. As Darrell said, we are free to fail, and fail gloriously. Our value is not derived from the outcome of our efforts. We are free from the task of controlling the future; the future is secure and our mission remains the same: to help this world become the home God intends his heirs to live in. We do not have to get ahead of the next trend or wave; we are free to enjoy the ride on whatever wave comes our way.

CHAPTER NINE

Home and Free

~

I've had the opportunity to visit the ruins of Priene, a town in what is the former Asia Minor, twice. Back in Paul's day, it was located on the Aegean Sea and had a good harbor. It was also located, to its advantage, in the Meander River Valley. It was an important, large town with a population of almost 40,000. I think Herod would have been impressed with Priene. One of his heroes, Alexander the Great, lived there for a brief time. Alexander funded the Temple of Athena in Priene—an architectural marvel. Herod would have appreciated how the temple used its power to promote the common good and simultaneously promote itself. The Temple to Athena provided water to travelers, food to the hungry, and free medical care to the ill. It even offered free daycare! Our guide, Ray VanderLaan, reminded us of the prevailing theory in this part of the ancient world: your god was judged by the temple the god had. Athena, a reflection of her temple, must surely have been both marvelous and generous! Herod, who was an apostle for Hellenistic culture in many ways, would have appreciated the strong

Hellenistic flavor of Preine. It also featured a temple to Zeus, which included a large agora (marketplace), a theater, and a stadium.

There was a small Jewish population living in Priene during Paul's lifetime. They were likely not allowed to vote in the town elections, nor were they allowed to buy or sell in the agora because they did not offer worship of incense to the gods of the town and the patron gods of the agora. The Jews were called "atheists" because of their refusal to worship the Greek and Roman gods. Herod would have likely been in favor of these tactics of official repression of the Jews. However, Preine, which was ninety percent pagan at one time, become ninety percent Christian within 125 years! David Bentley Hart writes in *Atheist Delusions*, "I am convinced that, given how radically at variance Christianity was with the culture it slowly and relentlessly displaced, its eventual victory was an event of such improbability as to strain the very limits of our understanding of historical causality" (xi). How did this amazing transformation take place in Rome and the rest of Asia Minor?

It is easier to define that which was not a factor of this amazing transformation than to define its cause. A Herodian style show of architectural extravagance was not the key factor of the Christian takeover; the first large buildings for Christian worship did not appear until the fourth century. Archaeologists in the early twentieth century discovered a small, home worship center in Priene. First thought to be a house church, it was later discovered that this single room was a small synagogue with a Torah closet and a carving of a menorah on the floor that in no way resembled a Herod-sized temple.

Herod also made great use of his political power and the alliances he made with the powerful rulers of his day. But, as previously noted, the Jews and Christians did not even have the right to vote, nor did they obtain the favor of local politicians in Priene. Herod had Antony, and later Octavian, to provide security for his kingdom; the Jews in Asia Minor had no such security in the first two centuries. Perhaps our current desire as Christians to impose our will in the political arena may be a sign of orphaned hearts rather than of faithful obedience to God; our "good and faithful" work seems to lack true faith when it is positioned side-by-side with the faithfulness of the Priene Christians.

The Christian community likely did not thrive by practicing some of the methods that we would consider vital to the spreading of

Christianity today. There is no record of a great preacher or Christian leader moving to Priene and conducting evangelistic crusades in the theater or stadium. The evangelistic paths of Paul, John, and Timothy can be traced as far as Ephesus but not all the way to Priene. Nor is the message of salvation in this community centered on going to heaven when you die. Almost every major religion in the Roman world promised salvation and a trip to heaven. Some even worshiped gods who died on behalf of the people. Miracles were also part of many religious narratives. "If you died tonight where would you go?" would have likely been answered by members of most major religions in the first and second century with the same exuberant exclamation as Christians answer today: “Heaven!” But the Christian community in Priene grew at an unbelievable rate. What caused this growth? What was so unique about the Christian community?

It would be appropriately biblical to say the rise of the Christian community in Priene was due to the risen Jesus and the power of the Holy Spirit. But how was Jesus experienced? How did the Spirit move in that place at that time? Vanderlaan postulates that the sense of community and extended family these Christians brought from their

Jewish heritage to Priene made the difference. Many scholars believe that the small synagogue discovered in Priene was located in the middle of a larger house that had rooms for fifty to 100 people. According to this theory, these Christians lived together in an extremely close community. They were unable to participate in the political process and in the marketplace, so they learned to depend on one another for survival. They developed a community and a sense of belonging that was never before experienced in the Hellenistic world.

The sense of family and belonging worked to undermine the rigid stratification of that Greco-Roman world. Hellenists would have been stunned to see a master serving a slave or the employee eating at the same time as the employer—both of which happened during the sacrament of the Eucharist. The feeling of community that the residents of Priene found in their contact with the Christian community stands in stark contrast to the large, impersonal, Herodian efforts of the community of faith in our contemporary world. This Richard Halverson quote, which I heard from Ray VanderLaan in 2008, sums it up: "When the church was primarily Jewish, it was a family. When it was primarily Greek, it became a philosophy. When it was primarily Roman, it became an organization. When it was primarily European, it became a culture, and when it was primarily American, it became a business."

The rise of Christianity in Priene also had to do with the fact that early Christians, like the Jews in that small house, lived in close proximity to the residents of Preine. They chose not to avoid the dominant culture; they lived among the non-Christian people and engaged them, but they did not fully assimilate into the Preine culture. Separatism remains a temptation to the Christian community today; we have our own schools, our own recording artists, and even our own code or language. These Priene Christians, however, did not need to remain isolated in order to preserve their Christian identity.

Complete assimilation is also a temptation today. We are confronted with the call to become one with the predominant culture in values and practices; we are tempted to fit in. American civil religion, "God and country," is a product of this desire. There is so much discussion about preserving our constitutional freedoms to include the practice of religion. Priene Christians had no such sanctioned freedoms. They chose to risk exclusion and death in order to practice their faith. They lived among the residents of Priene and exemplified the community of faith for them. They modeled love for God, love for one another, and love for the world that stood in amazing contrast to those who were outside the Judeo-Christian culture.

The care for the needy illustrated by the Christian community in Priene also set it apart in the pagan world. Rodney Stark, who has researched the rise of Christianity in the Roman Empire extensively, notes that the compassion and care extended by the Christians to people in need was a key factor in the rise of the faith in that region. When plagues hit ancient Rome and Alexandria, the wealthy and the educated people left town; anyone who could afford to leave got the you-know-what out of Dodge. But the Christians remained behind in the cities to care for the sick and dying—*all* of the sick and dying! This community care frustrated the aptly named Julian the Apostate, who sought to destroy Christianity and revive the pagan religion. He summed up it up as follows: "[What have] the Christians' benevolence to strangers, their care for the graves of the dead, and a pretended holiness of their lives...done the most to increase atheism? When the impious Galileans support not only their own poor but ours as well, all men see that our people lack aid from us."

Why I'm so interested in people who lived two thousand years ago in a town that no longer exists? I am interested because we live in a culture that is similar to the pagan culture in Priene. Though the majority of Americans would profess a belief in God, the dominant patterns of thought and behavior in our culture are as Hellenistic as they get. Hellenism can be described as a system that glorifies the human. Truly biblical Christianity seems to be a minority report today, but that is not all bad. It gives us a similar opportunity as our ancestors in Asia Minor had: by the witness of our lives, we can draw the notice of our world to our Rabbi and Lord, Jesus Christ.

My theory about what took place in Asia Minor, and what may be helpful to us today, is not grounded in a study of historical sites; it is grounded in my experience with people. I think the non-Christians in Priene were attracted to the same unique ways of being in the world illustrated by the Christians in Priene that attract to me to Jesus and his followers. In the Priene Christians, non-Christians saw an attractive display of freedom. Though they could have been considered the dispossessed and the oppressed due to their political and economic disadvantages, the Priene Christians lived as free heirs in the house of

God. In other words, they did not live out of the orphaned existence of the pagans scrambling for security and identity; they lived the free existence of the heir. That is, of course, my assumption, but this assumption is rooted in what I have seen and experienced living among Christian people who are trying to live this freedom. Living into our identities as heirs rather than orphans possesses great promise for the lives of individual Christians and our faith community as a whole, and it could become a powerful witness to our non-Christian, Prieneian-like-pagan contemporaries.

I experience freedom in three major areas when I live as an heir and not as an orphan:

Freedom from guilt of the past: Erma Bombeck famously noted that guilt is "the gift that keeps on giving." As a pastor, I have watched guilt paralyze people and keep them locked in the past. Rick Warren noted in 1995 that "you cannot relate to the present if you are busy reacting to the past." My own sense of guilt tends to show up as a voice of shame that reminds me of my past failures and insists that those failures indicate a current inadequacy to meet my present needs. That is my orphan shame voice. When I am living as a beloved son, I realize that no past event is going to remove me from my place in the family.

Freedom from fear in the present: Fear of rejection and failure has the greatest effect on my life. Having my home in my Father's house reminds me that even if I am rejected by some, I am accepted by God and by the other members of my family. Living honestly as an heir compels me to truthfully acknowledge that though I desire the approval of people, I do not need to tailor my actions to their wishes because I know their praises and criticisms do not affect my place in the house. An orphan lives in constant fear of rejection. That is a feeling that I am more than happy to remove from my consciousness.

Freedom from worry about the future: When my orphan heart cannot trust that I will have a place in the future, I have to try to manipulate and control the future. I can go through countless "what if" scenarios and make contingency plans regarding each scenario. As an heir, however, my future is secure. The Father holds it for me; my job is to discover and live into the future that God already has planned for me. Freedom from worry about the future gives me the freedom to live into the present. As I previously noted, the best things in my life came when I was not trying hard to secure my future—when I was living with the freedom of an heir.

As we live lives of freedom in the midst of people who struggle as orphans with the unmet need for home, acceptance, and a sense of value, we will find that people are drawn to us. However, if we, using the orphan methods of coercion, persuasion, and extravagance, try to reach out to others, we may fall like Herod in complete destruction, collapse, and irrelevance. In our effort to become relevant, we work against our relevance. It is the hope, joy, love, and peace we exemplify as heirs to the Kingdom of God that makes us relevant. As people experience these things it our midst, a new Priene-style Christian community will arise. People will be drawn to the promise of *home* we share in our Father's house—a promise that frees us from fear, guilt, shame, and worry and blesses us beyond our wildest dreams.

EPILOGUE

The Two Tombs

~

Some of our leaders traveled to Israel on a tour led by Pastor Scott. Matt, one of our other pastors, had a realization on the last day of the trip:

> After a long journey of eleven days hiking through the desert, through the towns surrounding the Sea of Galilee, and through the historic sites of Jerusalem, we came to the Herodium. We had visited Herod's palaces at Masada and Caesarea Maritima. We saw the grander with which Herod built and learned of his vast wealth and engineering feats—a freshwater pool in the Mediterranean Sea, pools in the desert, etc. Herod had extreme wealth and knowledge and learned to harness nature and create his own majesty where nature would not allow it.

But Herod built selfishly. He killed many members of his family, focused only on himself, and protected his wealth over everything else. He feared the people around him would turn on him. Knowing no one would mourn his death, he ordered his commanders to hold leaders hostage and kill them after his death to ensure that people would mourn on the day he died.

We came to the Herodium, a palace in the desert, where Herod literally moved a mountain to build his palace in a place where no one could reach him. Herod changed the landscape of nature; he tried to play God, displaying his own power and protecting himself from others. We climbed to the top of the mountain to see the palace where Herod supposedly spent most of his time. On the way down, we came to Herod's tomb.

The recently discovered tomb is large and very well-built; like most of Herod's structures, it is a tribute to himself. As we stood at the tomb, our leader asked us what we were thinking. We reflected on how all of

Herod's palaces, while majestic in their day, had crumbled to ruins; some were destroyed not long after his rule ended. The massive structures he spent his time and fortune assembling were toppled and torn down by the next regime of power. Caesarea Maritima was destroyed by nature itself; the raw force of the sea still throws the castle's granite and marble up onto the shore to this day. All of Herod's massive empire, held together by fear, force, and rule, crumbled soon after his death. The ways of the world crumble without the drive and determination to hold them up, while God's nature merely ebbs and flows to overcome all Herod built in resistance to it.

Then Stefanie mentioned the fact that Herod's tomb was only recently discovered. This powerful ruler's majestic tomb, a tribute to his life, was hidden for thousands of years. It was discovered in a time when no one could remember or celebrate him. We were alone on our visit to this forgotten tomb. The day before, however, we stood in a long line at the church of the Holy Sepulcher to visit Jesus' tomb. Jesus' tomb was donated; it was not built specifically to celebrate His life. He led by support, not by force; he led with love, not selfish grander. He was a willing sacrifice, not a fearful victim of disease.

People came from all over the world to visit the places Jesus visited in life in Jerusalem and other cities in Israel. The number of His followers continues to grow because He left His mark by love, sacrifice, and grace; Herod tried to leave his mark through fear, force, and personal power, but he was left in ruins with no one to uphold his legacy.

We stood in the palace of Herod, meeting power rotted by time and abandoned by the world. We couldn't help but think of the love, respect, and faith shown by the followers of Jesus who still visit his simple-looking tomb. The contrast between the way Herod lived and the way

Jesus lived and the different fruit that each life yielded was chilling.

The difference is indeed chilling, but it is also inviting. If we, like Jesus, can live as beloved children, exuding freedom from guilt, fear, and worry, and participating in generous acts that contribute to the restoration of God's plan for all creation, people may once again line up to join us in this adventure.

~

READING LIST

~

- *Experiencing God* by Henry Blackaby
- *Daring Greatly* by Brene Brown
- *Opening Blind Eyes* by John Claypool
- *Spiritual Slavery To Spiritual Sonship* by Jack Frost
- *Atheist Delusions: The Christian Revolution and Its Fashionable Enemies* by David Bentley Hart
- *The Leader's Journey* by Jim Herrington
- *To Change The World: The Irony, Tragedy, & Possibility of Christianity in the Late Modern World* by James Davison Hunter
- *Home Tonight* by Henri Nouwen
- *The Jesus Way* by Eugene H. Peterson
- *Herod King of the Jews and Friend of the Romans* by Peter Richardson
- *Falling Upward* by Richard Rohr
- *A Culture of Honor* by Denny Silk
- *Slow Church* by Christian C. Smith and John Pattison
- *The New Parish* by Paul Sparks and Dwight J. Friessen
- *From Orphans to Heirs* by Mark Stibbe
- *I am Your Father* by Mark Stibbe
- *From Jesus to Christianity* by L. Michael White
- *The Divine Conspiracy* by Dallas Willard
- *Simply Christian* by N.T. Wright
- *Surprised by Hope* by N.T. Wright
- *Simply Jesus* by N.T. Wright

ABOUT THE AUTHOR

David McNitzky has been the senior pastor at Alamo Heights United Methodist Church in San Antonio for the past 20 years. He was previously the senior pastor at the First United Methodist Church in Boerne (1988-1995), the pastor at the Helotes Hills United Methodist Church (1983-1988), and the pastor at the Los Fresnos United Methodist Church (1980-1983).

Reverend McNitzky and his spouse Pamela have three sons: Mark, Ryan, and Reed.

Contact information:

Reverend David J. McNitzky (Pamela)
Alamo Heights United Methodist Church
825 East Basse Road
San Antonio, TX 78209

OFFICE: 210/826-3215
Assistant: Leah Jayne

FAX: 210/826-3897

E-MAIL: dmcnitzky@ahumc.org or LJayne@ahumc.org

53099153R00114

Made in the USA
San Bernardino, CA
06 September 2017